Olly Murs
Happy Days

PHOTOGRAPHY BY DEAN FREEMAN

Olly Murs
Happy Days

WITH MARTIN ROACH / PHOTOGRAPHY AND
CREATIVE DIRECTION BY DEAN FREEMAN

Introduction

I am standing alone in an enormous, spotlessly clean garage, part of a multi-million-dollar luxury mansion in Los Angeles. On one side of me is the world's most expensive car, a £1 million Bugatti. Nearby is a sparkling Rolls-Royce Phantom, gleaming under the lights. I'm stood at the end of a long walkway that will take me out of Simon Cowell's garage and into his beautifully manicured gardens, where he will tell me if I have made it through to the Live Finals of *The X Factor* ... or not.

I'm the last contestant to find out my fate and it seems to take an eternity to be called, by which time I am having a mild panic attack, crying, hyperventilating, my heart's pounding, I am losing my breath... I am proper nervous.

This is the biggest moment of my life. As I stand there struggling for breath, I really feel that this one moment could change my life. I start talking to myself out loud, calming myself down, going through the whole scenario like some split personality. I feel like I am going bonkers, standing alone for ages in that garage in LA, in a world that is a million miles away from home, waiting for my life to be affected in such a massive way by someone else's decision.

A few minutes later I am called through and there is Simon, sitting in front of me, telling me the reasons behind his decision. As I stand there trying not to shake with emotion, he says, 'Olly, you are a risk ... it is as simple as that.'

from top, l-r: Aged 3 at the caravan we stayed at in Cornwall; With my mates on a pre-V Festival camping trip; Winning the Essex Braintree league, 2007; A fancy dress party – wearing my dads 70's outfit; Christmas 2008 with the family after coming back from Australia; Messing around at the zoo in Australia; Me and my twin brother playing football against each other at school; At Butlins sporting my David Beckham haircut; Playing the guitar to my mates who are oblivious I have just got through to X Factor Bootcamp; Dancing around at a mate's wedding reception; 'The Smalltown Blaggers' performing at my dad's 50th birthday party in our back garden; After winning £10 on Deal or No Deal in 2007 – why do I look so happy?; Walking around London and randomly seeing my album advert on a bus; At Radio 1 after getting my first No.1 with 'Please Don't Let Me Go'; Returning to the XF studios in 2011, sitting in Simon's famous chair; Messing around in a Rihanna cardboard cut out.

5

I remember those crazy, intense events in LA like they happened yesterday. I can still feel the raw emotion as I stood there in front of Simon, waiting. But I can also still remember what it felt like just a couple of years earlier, when my life was drifting and I had no direction, when I went to work each day feeling like I was just going through the motions. When my childhood dreams as well as my more recent ambitions had been scuppered and I was struggling to explain to people why I kept trying, even though I just seemed to be going nowhere. Something had to change in my life.

From 2007 onwards, my life has been a non-stop roller coaster of extreme emotions, crazy days and unexpected highs, but my life hasn't been without its lows either. In this book I've tried to picture myself sitting down with you, the reader, explaining what I was thinking and feeling during those times, and hopefully giving you a fly-on-the-wall view of my amazing journey into a place where I finally found what had been missing all those years: music.

1. Because You're Young

Where I used to live in Witham, Essex, pretty much all of the family lived nearby. Both my nans lived really close, my aunties and uncles too, so they were always coming round or we were round theirs. It was exciting as a kid, it felt like every week was a party. It wasn't, of course, but my mum's side of the family in particular were party animals, so we'd have these get-togethers all the time. My nan and Mum used to throw great parties, especially on New Year's Eve, and there'd always be karaoke.

When you look at my family's history, singing and performing have always been in the blood, I guess. My great auntie Pat was a professional singer in the West End, my nan herself used to sing at gentlemen's country clubs and on my dad's side they always used to enter amateur dancing competitions, though really more as a hobby. But going even further back than that, my great-great-gran was part of the biggest circus in Latvia during the 1930s, performing trapeze and tightrope, which is pretty amazing really!

Mum and Dad would always have music on in the house, so they used to get me and my twin brother Ben, plus our sister Fay, up singing. We used to love it. Grandad was the first in the family to get a video camera, so he and my parents have got loads of home videos of us lot dancing around. We were like little performing monkeys but it's really good when you watch 'em back, and we're lucky to have that footage. We used to play Michael Jackson so much in the house growing up. My brother used to pretend he was MJ and we'd be his backing dancers. So in a strange way it feels like ever since I was a kid I've been in front of a camera performing. All them elements put together – the circus performers, the West End and club singing, the dance competitions, the karaoke parties, happy times with us three singing at home – I wouldn't say they made me what I am today, but I think it's where I got my instinct to perform.

Growing up I was into a lot of different bands. My parents were always listening to something so I would hear Bowie, the Smiths, the Jam, loads of

Madness, Weller, Michael Jackson, Stevie Wonder, James Brown. As I grew up, I was kind of a Spice Girls fan, which my dad was worried about! A lot of boy bands too – Blue, Five, Westlife – but I also loved Blur and Oasis. I liked all sorts of stuff.

But as a kid music wasn't my first love. As far back as 1990, when I was six, it was football, football, football. I was a striker and played every day – when I got older I would train every day too, and that was the case right through into my early twenties. I was massively into Man United. I was an avid fan, so I had the wallpaper, the United pillows and duvet set, posters, mugs, the lot!

I wanted to be a professional footballer. That's what every kid's dream was. My uncle, John Pollard, used to play professional football for Colchester United, so from a young age it seemed that a career in football was a possibility. My schoolteachers would ask what I wanted to do as a job. My first answer would always be 'Professional footballer, sir.' Apart from football I didn't really know what else to try. So between the ages of sixteen and nineteen I went and did a college course, an NVQ in Sport and Recreation, plus Personal Training, for three years.

So although music was a constant feature in my house, pretty much soundtracking my childhood and always in the back of my mind, I never thought for the life of me that I'd be a pop star. I was always performing and having a laugh with my family, but as a kid it never crossed my mind that singing could be a career; football was my thing.

Funnily enough, before I went off to college, a lot of people at school wrote in my 'End of Year' book that they really hoped I had a career in music and singing. Every day I'd sing at school, walking around with my mates, or even on my own walking down the corridor. Looking back, I suppose I was singing all the time. To be honest, I was only having a laugh. I enjoyed it but I never sang in front of anyone properly. I just kept it quiet. It was bubbling inside, at the back of my mind, but I just left it there. Where I live in Essex, unless you know people in the industry, there's no way you'll ever find out how to break into the music business.

When I was a teenager at college, *Pop Idol* was on and I can remember enjoying watching Gareth Gates and Will Young battling it out, but my head was still full of succeeding in football, so I didn't really think much else about it. But when *The X Factor* started a few years later in 2004, that was the first time I was like, *Wow, what a great programme to go on! These kids are singing in front of these famous judges with a chance to win a £1 million record contract. Happy days!* It was the first time I'd seen people come from families with absolutely no contacts in the music business – like mine – and end up in the charts. I thought some of the contestants on *The X Factor* were so good that they had to be from stage school, but I soon realised they weren't, they were just ordinary people giving it a go. That was the very first inkling of me wondering if singing or performing could be something more than just having a great time with family or mates.

After college I was in and out of jobs all the time, but I was a very good worker and I've always had a great work ethic. Ever since I'd got my first paper round at fourteen – I eventually did three paper rounds a week – I'd grafted. From a young age my parents told me that nothing comes to you for free, you have to work for it. Graft, graft, graft. So it's always been in my blood to give 110 per cent. I would go on to work in sales, recruitment, mortgage selling, data entry (just typing in catalogue numbers *all* day!), on a clothing manufacturer's production line, loads of industrial factory jobs. I even worked in a jam factory! You name it, I've probably done it.

Obviously none of these jobs was my ideal career. I was just moving from one temporary job to the next for much of my early twenties, earning some money but not really loving anything I was doing. I just felt there was more to life than the nine-to-five. The problem was, I didn't know what that 'missing' part was, so for a while there I was kinda drifting a little.

Like I said, I'd never sung in front of an audience at this stage. I'd only ever done karaoke at home and occasionally with a few mates round too. Nothing serious. Then for some reason in May 2007 – I had just turned twenty-three – I thought I'd have a go at *The X Factor. Why not? It'll be a laugh!* I just fancied having a go, so I got the phone number online and went along to the producers' auditions in London. I stood in those long queues along with hundreds of other people, put on my number, then when it came to my turn I took up my position in front of three producers that I'd never seen before who worked on the show. I nervously sang 'I Wanna Be Like You' from *The Jungle Book* and got a 'No' straight away. At that point I didn't really mind, because it was as much for the crack as anything. But I wasn't done with *The X Factor* yet...

2. Little By Little

In the late summer of 2007, I'd just split up with my first girlfriend and was pretty down, so Mum had sent off for an application form for me to be a contestant on Noel Edmonds' show, *Deal Or No Deal*, which had a top prize of £250,000. We always watched it together and I'd say, 'Wouldn't it be great to go on there, Mum!' Well, we applied, I got the call for an audition and they must have liked what they saw because I got invited to appear on the show. At the time I did *Deal Or No Deal* I was a recruitment consultant.

I wasn't fame hungry: I did that show for the money. I wanted to get some cash behind me because Mum was quite ill at the time. We weren't really sure what was the matter with her, so it was all very worrying. I thought if I could win a good chunk of cash I could sort Mum out and maybe even put a deposit down on a house. My nan always wanted to go to Graceland in Vegas and I could've took her there too perhaps, so I was really focused on coming home with a big prize. I still hadn't found much direction in my career, so I felt like this was a real chance to do something with my life.

On the day of filming, I couldn't believe it when I was actually picked out to play. It's an amazing feeling. I did a little Michael Jackson moonwalk on to the centre of the stage and I really enjoyed being there. Noel was really supportive and the other contestants were great too; they really wanted me to do well.

Initially it was going quite well but I said, 'No Deal' to an offer of £26,000 from the Banker and after that it all started to go horribly wrong. In quick succession I took out four big money boxes in a row, first £250,000, then £75,000, £35,000 and finally £100,000. Suddenly that left me with just £10,000 or £1000. The Banker offered me £1000 but I just thought, *Nah, let's just go for it!* Then the £10,000 went as well! I was offered £450, but I still went for it, 'cos I was down to either £10 or £1000. As Noel started to open the final box, he said,

'Did the bad luck go on for ever?'

Yes, it did, 'cos I won just £10. I was absolutely gutted.

Noel was really nice, saying, 'Olly, every now and again we meet a special person on this show and you do not have "Failure" written all over you. It's been a pleasure to meet you and I'm gonna miss you!' He also said it was one of the unluckiest games he'd ever seen. That was all really nice of him to say, but to be honest I was totally gutted.

It was hard, going home with a tenner. I walked away from that experience with some positives – I did have an amazing time, I met some amazing people, including a girl called Kate who worked on the show that I'm still friends with to this day – but there were a lot of negatives too. Backstage after the show I was sat there with a couple of contestants who'd won £25,000 and £16,000, really big sums, but I'd be sitting on a bus home the next day with a tenner. Worse still, they gave me a certificate but I had to wait for the cheque! There's a *Deal Or No Deal* tradition that if someone wins less than £100, the other contestants have a whip-round and chip in, which they did for me. That raised about £480, which was really kind.

I remember going back to the hotel that night and trudging into the bathroom, where I just cried, all this emotion came flooding out. That was only for a few short minutes, but it had been such an emotional day. I know it's only a game show yet it really hurt me. I so badly wanted to win some money, because I just felt that could've changed my life. And I'd turned down twenty-six grand.

I remember phoning my family and Mum was like, 'No, you are joking, Olly, you're winding us up!' That was really hard, replying, 'Mum, I'm being deadly serious, I've won a tenner!' I felt like I'd let them down. Then I came home and waited a couple of months for the show to be aired, and in the meantime all my mates were guessing what I'd won. I told them I'd only won a tenner but they didn't believe me! Then the show came on and it got into the local press and radio. 'Local boy on TV wins £10!', all that.

That was my first taste of how being on TV can sometimes be negative. I'd be walking down the streets of Witham and lads would shout, 'Oi, are you that bloke that only won a tenner! Ha ha!' They would be laughing in my face, gesturing at me. Down the pub people made me feel really uncomfortable too, you could hear them sniggering, 'That's the geezer off the telly. What a prat, what a plonker, what an idiot.'

Don't get me wrong: it wasn't the end of the world not winning some money on the show. I had a decent enough job, it paid okay, but I just really wanted to move on with my life. I was a little bit older than a couple of my mates but they had girlfriends, jobs that were paying more money than mine, they had better cars than me, they had houses, they were settling down and I just felt I needed a bit of a helping hand. *Deal Or No Deal* was gonna be that helping hand. If I'd won some money I would've thought, *Right, I'm moving now, I feel good. I've got things going on.* But I didn't, I won a tenner, which is why I was so upset and down about it. It was a kick in the nuts.

I was twenty-three with no real career prospects and no sense of where I was going. I certainly didn't have a job that felt like it was the career I wanted to do for the rest of my life. The nasty comments round Witham only lasted a couple of weeks and I soon bounced back. So after *Deal Or No Deal* I threw myself back into football. It was still something that I loved and was really passionate about. I played Saturday matches and Sunday league too; when I wasn't playing football I was watching it on telly and on Sunday evenings I even played with some mates just for fun in a five-a-side team. By my early twenties, I was a decent standard and I was getting paid around £30 a game playing semi-professionally for my local team, Witham Town Football Club. If I was honest with myself, I knew I wasn't going to make it to the top leagues by then because at twenty-three I was already much older than lads who were playing full-time professionally. You see these kids who are snapped up by seventeen, so it wasn't really gonna happen for me at that level.

But that didn't mean I couldn't make some kind of career out of football – even if it wasn't professionally. After the huge disappointment of *Deal Or No Deal*, I thought, *I'll get back to football, get scoring goals again, get back with the lads, have a bit of a crack.* I was really looking forward to it. I got my fitness back, started playing and quickly scored a couple of goals. But I was about to have another stroke of bad luck...

One Sunday night we were playing this game and losing 2–0. Midway through the first half I went running after the ball and suddenly, without warning, my left knee buckled behind me. At that moment I thought I'd broken my leg. I hobbled back to the dressing room. My leg was really sore and had already started to blow up, so I could hardly walk on it. I was supposed to be going round to a girl's house that night, and I was looking forward to seeing her, so despite my knee being so swollen I somehow got in the car and drove round to hers, but by the end of the night I could only just put enough pressure on the clutch to change gear and get home.

I knew I'd done something really bad, so I went to see the physio at the club. He iced it up and told me to rest for two weeks, then reassess. I did that and the swelling went down really well. It quickly felt much better and I was optimistic it had repaired itself, but when I went to play a few weeks later it happened again. Every couple of months this would happen: I'd get injured, rest up, start playing again and then the knee would go. Eventually I went to the doctor and he said I'd torn my cruciate ligament. He explained that there was an operation to repair the injury but there was a two-year waiting list. I was like, 'Are you having a laugh? Two years?' At that point I couldn't think of anything worse. Two years off football would've felt like an eternity.

That was a low point. I'd just done *Deal Or No Deal*, that had gone tits up, I'd split up with my girlfriend, I didn't enjoy my job, and now this had happened it looked like I was going to lose football too. I couldn't wait two years, so I took the quicker alternative, which was to have the knee 'flushed out'. After some rest and physio to build the knee back up, they told me 'you can hopefully play again at a decent level.' They did however warn me that even after this more minor operation, my knee would always be really weak.

Even so, I had the knee flushed out and started the slow process of building up my fitness again. The problem was that football was my social life too: at weekends, before and after matches, training in the week, that was my social circle. I'd never been one for going out drinking, that wasn't my cup of tea, but now I wasn't playing at all while I recuperated, I started to go to the pub more. I was pretty low and just sitting at home wasn't gonna help, so I preferred to go down the pub and hang out with the lads down there. It had been a crappy year. I kept a happy front up for the lads but the start of 2008 was definitely a low period.

The pub I used to go to was called the George in Witham. It was a decent place with some great regulars, although sometimes there'd be a few blokes go in there looking for fights. But 90 per cent of the punters were brilliant, proper geezers, proper lads I'd get on well with, nice old men and women too, some really interesting characters. On Sunday nights there was never anyone in there, though. I was chatting to the landlord, John Fisher, one Sunday when it was really quiet and I noticed a karaoke machine in the corner. I asked him about it and he explained it was all wired up and ready to go. I'd loved doing karaoke at home and I always used to dance and perform when us lads would go out clubbing. I was a bit of a joker: I'd pretend to do the MC Hammer dance, show them the MJ moves that me and my brother used to do (they became quite legendary in Witham stag do's!) and I was quite good at impressions too – I could do a decent Shaggy, you know, Mr Boombastic. I did this silly Spanish accent too. But this was all just having a laugh, fooling about with my mates. I'd never once go up and sing in front of anyone in public.

For some reason on this Sunday night in the George, I just fancied a go. I'd had a few drinks and I thought, *Sod it! Why not?* So I got up and started singing. Looking back, this was quite a big deal.

I just started singing for a laugh, thinking that other people would soon get up and join in. After a few songs everyone seemed to be enjoying it and they kept requesting more songs and somehow it kinda turned into a little gig. A few of the other lads got up and done a couple of songs, I did a couple of jokes and impressions too, and everyone was laughing. It was a great night!

We started going down the George every Sunday and doing the same thing, singing, having a laugh, people were joining in, it was just good fun. At that point it was just whoever turned up and fancied joining in, nothing formal. By February, John took me to one side and said, 'We should do a proper karaoke night every Sunday. I'll give you some money, let's give it a go.' He was paying me thirty or forty quid a night, it was a laugh and I enjoyed it for a while. It started to get a bit repetitive after a few weeks, though, and I did stop for a while, but John said he was missing me, so I started going again and loads of people were always coming along. However, I soon started to get bored again, so one night I took John to one side and said, 'I'm gonna knock this on the head, John...'

I knew he'd be disappointed but instead he said, 'Olly, look, I really think you are a great entertainer, a really good singer. I really enjoy your company, you're a great guy to have in the pub, you have a laugh with people, and I'd love you to do a proper gig of your own down here.'

'Really? Are you having a laugh?'

'Trust me,' he said. 'I've seen loads of bands come down here and perform and you are better than all of them. Come and do a gig!'

That was the first time that anyone outside of my family had ever said to me that I could sing. No one ever said, 'You've got a really good voice, you could do this, Olly.' So I never really had much self-belief. I felt that I had a raw talent, I had something that was positive, but no one had ever really said such a thing to me direct, until John spoke to me that night.

I was amazed and really excited, so when he said he'd pay me £200 cash for a gig on Easter Bank Holiday weekend a couple of months later, I was like, 'Oh my days! Yes!' I pointed out to him that I didn't have any kind of band and he gave me the number of a local guitarist, John Goodey. I gave John the guitarist a buzz – I knew some of his brothers through football – then went round his house and me and Johnny Boy hit it off immediately. We started getting a few songs together and then a set list. It was wicked, so exciting!

Easter came and we did a pre-gig rehearsal round Mum and Dad's house, then on the actual night the gig itself was great! Performing with John in the band gave me something to focus on too, a hobby, something to feel passionate about. We called ourselves the Smalltown Blaggers and started doing other gigs around pubs in Witham, some parties – we did a couple of eighteenths and a few weddings – we were just doing cover versions, but it was working well. Happy days!

When May came round I decided that I fancied another crack at *The X Factor*. I'd been singing much more this time so my confidence was up, I was starting to think that I could really enjoy being proper involved in music in some way, although I wasn't really sure how that could happen yet. So I went along to the auditions again. I made the same journey into town, stood in the same long queues, took my number just like I had the year before and positioned myself in front of three producers who, again, I didn't recognise. This time I sang Paolo Nutini's 'Last Request'.

And I got the same answer.

Another 'no'.

3. The Great Escape

I loved my football but I was still struggling to come back from the injury. I really enjoyed singing with John at the few pubs and events around Witham as the Smalltown Blaggers too, but I wasn't really into my job; it was okay but it was just something I did to earn a few quid. What I did earn I'd been saving 'cos my New Year's resolution for 2008 had been to get a bit of cash behind me. By the late summer, when I looked at my bank account there was about three or four grand in there, so that was when I made a decision that I will always be glad of: I decided to go travelling!

I just wanted to get away. Even though I was enjoying being in the band with John, it was still a tough time. The problem was that my life was like a bubble and it felt very frustrating. Everything seemed mapped out for me: I was gonna live in Essex, meet a girl who lived down the road from me, we were gonna get married, have kids, I was gonna be in a job that I didn't quite enjoy, we might move somewhere else but we might not, then I'd watch my grandkids grow up, then eventually I'd snuff it! That's all I could see but it was also everything I didn't want; that's not a dig at that way of life, it's just not what I wanted to do at that point. When I was growing up, it was all about what you drove, what you wore, how big your house was, but I always felt a little bit different. I always stayed clear of the kind of girls who were just after the flash cars. Never really my cup of tea. I just felt like there was more to life outside of that bubble.

I'd done a couple of lads' holidays but I hadn't travelled the world. That's why I decided that travelling further afield was something I wanted to do. Quit my job, be a bit spontaneous for once, travel to Australia, clear my head a little bit and come back fresh with some new ideas and then who knows? Maybe new opportunities might pop up? I just needed to change my life a little bit, take it in another direction, stop being 'safe'…

So I did quit my job, then I booked a flight for September and went and told my parents. You can imagine their reaction: it was like, 'What the hell are you doing? I explained why I wanted to do the trip and although they didn't really agree, they did understand.

Having said all that, there was a part of me that was like, *Am I just being a dickhead? This is just not a realistic dream, me travelling, going to Australia.* I wondered if I should stay at home and slug it out, get a nice car, a decent job, see where that took me. But I just couldn't face that. I hadn't got any sense of direction, I just didn't feel happy, even when I was out with my mates and having a party, I wasn't proper happy...

It might sound like I am contradicting myself when I say I didn't feel like I was running away from my problems, but I did need to make a drastic change. I felt very claustrophobic living that life in Witham. I don't judge people who live that lifestyle, absolutely not, everyone is different, different strokes for different folks, and if we were all the same it'd be boring. I was just looking at it thinking, *This can't be it for me.*

That's why travelling appealed to me. I was just searching for a change. I felt like something was missing. I didn't know it yet, but the part of me that was missing turned out to be music and singing, that was my change. It sounds so cheesy when you say it like that, but that's how it was. That was all still to come, though...

So anyway, I'd handed in my notice and had to start packing for three months' travelling around Australia. I was so excited. Mum and Dad were obviously a bit worried: they wanted to know if I was coming back to any job, how I was going to pay my way once I'd returned. They didn't want to see me drift, I guess, which is fair enough. My flight home was Christmas Eve, so I'd already got some gigs booked over the festive period, and the job agency I worked for said they could always get me something. But at that point I didn't want to think about working in Witham again; that was what I was flying to Australia to get away from.

Another reason for wanting to make a change was that I'd been unlucky in love as well. I hadn't really met anyone that I loved. I'd had a couple of up-and-down relationships, a couple of girls who let me down who I'd really fancied, and then I got quite into this girl called Kate, who I'd met when she was working on *Deal Or No Deal.* She was a bit of a free spirit and I loved the fact that she had this amazing job travelling all over the UK, and she was also really into travelling overseas too. She was a major reason why I started thinking about travelling myself, and she gave my situation a completely different perspective. That relationship hadn't really worked out but I'd heard she was in Australia, so as well as going over there to clear my head, I'll be truthful and say I was also searching for this girl that I really liked. But that was a bit of a disaster because on the day I was flying to Oz, I found out that Kate had just come back to the UK!

I still got on the plane regardless. I knew I had to. That trip wasn't just about Kate, there were so many different reasons why I went over there. I needed direction, I needed to change my life, start from scratch again. That's what Australia represented for me: the chance to evaluate where I was going and what I wanted to do.

I really planned the trip, I'd booked my hostels, I knew where I was going, knew where I was staying... There was an old football pal of mine who used to fancy my sister who'd moved to Australia to change his life; he was in Melbourne and another one of my mates was in Brisbane. Kate had given me loads of stuff about places to go to too, good hostels and all that.

So I filled this really small backpack with just the essentials: I took a phone-charger but no laptop, a shaver, hardly any clothes. Looking back now I don't know how I managed with so little but it was exciting. It was the start of an adventure! The night before I went to stay at my sister's near Heathrow. I hadn't seen her for a while so that was great, and the next morning when she drove me to the airport she was crying, bless her!

I'd never been on a long-haul flight before: the furthest I'd ever been was to Egypt. Now all of a sudden I'm alone on a twenty-three-hour flight. I got my window seat and discovered that each passenger had this TV system like Sky+ where you can watch anything you want, when you want. Happy days! I was well chuffed! There was a nice pillow and I got myself a bit of kip. I didn't think too much about the impending trip at first.

Then we got to Hong Kong and the connecting flight wasn't for another six hours. If you know me then you'll know the best thing I can do is sleep. God, I love my sleep! So I just lay down on this row of chairs and tried to kip some more but I woke up after a while and there were still hours and hours left to go. I felt like Tom Hanks in *Terminal*; it was just the longest time. That's when I suddenly thought, *Jesus, what the hell am I doing?*

When I walked out at Sydney airport, it was a beautiful sunny day and I got a taxi to the hostel I was booked into. I quickly made friends with some fellow travellers and from then on we went out every day, there was so much to see. I quickly forgot about all my worries back at home and just had the best time ever. I was a typical young lad, I met girls along the way, a few girls I had fun with and slept with. I had a really good time. I spent three months in Australia and in many ways it was the best time of my life. I did all the tourist stuff like Bondi Beach, went to Brisbane to see my mate, then travelled up the east coast all on my own. It was incredible and I met some fantastic people.

Although being away had certainly lifted my spirits and I was having a great time, I obviously kept thinking about what I was gonna do if I returned to Essex. I used to sit on the beach and write down on a bit of paper what I wanted to do … what was the first thing that came into my mind? Someone told me to draw a line down the middle of the page, then list what I wanted do and what I didn't want to do, in each half.

The column of things I didn't want to do was pretty long and each time I would alter what came first, as there were quite a few things that I wasn't keen on: I didn't wanna do recruitment, I didn't wanna do office work, sell mortgage advice, sales, and I even came to realise that football was no longer an option as a career. However, every time I drew up a column of what I wanted to do, the first thing I would write down was 'Music and Singing'.

Every time.

With football gone, that was the only thing I had in my life that I loved and could think about doing in the future.

When it came to the day to fly home, I'd had such a fantastic time that – like many travellers – I was determined to return to Australia at some point. Just before I was due to leave, I was chatting to a mate of mine called Matty B and he was like, 'You wanna leave this paradise and go home to England when you are not even sure what you wanna do?' He said he could help me get a proper visa so I could stay longer, but I had something on my mind that had kept nagging me throughout my stay in Australia. Something that just wouldn't go away, something that I still had to do back at home.

One final *X Factor* audition…

4. Tomorrow's Just Another Day

After I came back from Australia, I started singing in the band with John again. We did a couple of gigs, including my dad's fiftieth-birthday party, various shows here and there, then I got asked to perform alongside a female vocalist for a band called F2K, a seven-piece that performed Motown songs at corporate events and bigger shows than I was used to with John.

I was still trying to find my way in music. I'd been to a lot of beaches in Australia and at every one there would be an Australian guy playing a guitar with all these birds around him; he could be the ugliest guy for miles around, yet every night there he was, pulling birds. So I'd decided that when I got back home I'd get a guitar and learn to play. I wanted to be that guy! Back in Essex, I was put in touch with a guitar tutor and I got seriously into practising, for hours on end. I just felt it was essential for me to play guitar to move my music forward, and besides, if that didn't work out and I went back to Australia, then at least I could be that guy on the beach!

The X Factor was always in the back of my mind: before I went to Australia, when I was sitting on all those beaches Down Under, and still, when I came back from travelling, there it was. I'd watched that show for years by now and failed twice already but I still felt that if I just had one more chance... I knew I was a good performer, I felt like I had a half-decent voice, so if I could just get in front of that judging panel, I could potentially change my life. I honestly believed if I could just get in front of Simon Cowell...

Initially when I came home from Australia, I was buzzing. It was great to be back, and I had all these stories to tell, I felt re-energised, I felt like my life had changed, I felt like I had achieved something. No one in my family had travelled to Australia before; most of my friends hadn't either. I showed the family and my friends my pictures and so for the first three or four weeks it was amazing.

I also had loads of gigs to do, and I had a bit of money coming in from various temp jobs – I worked as a receptionist in the local NHS, I got a job punching data in for orders from newspaper adverts for seeds, and that's also when I had a short spell working in a jam factory.

I did that for a few months. It was getting me through, I was paying my mum rent and my bills, plus saving a bit of money here and there. But then the excitement of Australia started to fade, that honeymoon period of being back began to wear off. It had made me feel like my life was interesting for a while but now it wasn't interesting any more, it was stagnant and I was working nine to five all over again.

At one point I was only working three days a week and that caused loads of arguments at home. I was having rows with Mum and Dad on a regular basis about me wanting to be a pop star, a singer, wanting to get into music. They were worried I'd wasted three years of college and I was struggling to pay them each week. It was getting really hard. Everything was just getting on top of me. I was like, 'Honestly, Mum, just bear with me on this one, it will all work out.'

Every Easter we have dinner at my nan's and everyone is there, the whole family. This particular year I was chatting to my uncle, I was a bit depressed, telling him I was thinking of doing *The X Factor* again. That show had sort of become a bad word with my family, who were like, 'Really? Come on, Olly, get realistic, you gotta get a good job now,' which was fair enough. I got that, I understood their reservations, because being a pop star isn't the sort of job you can just get from applying with a CV!

Then my grandad – Pop – came in and sat down and he was like, 'What are we talking about?' So we told him and then he said, 'You've got nothing, have you?'

I was obviously a bit taken aback. 'What?'

'Well, you've got nothing, have you, Olly? Nothing. You're mid-twenties, still living at home with your parents, no money in your account. When I was your age I had a mortgage, kids, a good job, a wife, a car, a good life... You've got nothing.'

'All right, that's a bit harsh!'

'Well, I need to tell you, Olly, you need a kick up the arse. You've got nothing. I didn't wanna say it but I had to 'cos you are my grandchild. Everyone else is beating round the bush but I'm not gonna do that.'

In a sense it was the most hurtful thing anyone's ever told me in my life...
But it was the truth.

Pop was dead right and the truth really, *really* hurt. After that conversation, I almost felt like I couldn't look him in the eye, as he'd really hit a nerve. I walked out that day and I didn't even say goodbye to him. I knew he didn't mean harm by it and when I talked to him afterwards I think he felt bad. But I'm glad he said it. I needed that conversation: Grandad saying those things was a real eye-opener for me.

I knew I had my third audition coming up for *The X Factor* and after what Pop had said to me I was like, *This is the last time I'm gonna do this show, I'm never gonna do it again.* My confidence was still only mediocre; in my head I was already planning what I was gonna do after the audition: I'd got a part-time job lined up in an insurance company. If I'd failed again, I would've walked away, not from music, but from *The X Factor.* I would've perhaps tried a different angle, maybe more gigs with John, maybe even Butlins, or perhaps gone to college to study music. As I waited for the audition day to arrive, I said to myself that I'd forget *The X Factor* once and for all if I got another 'No'. Hundred per cent.

Auditions are a very harsh process. For me, what's really hurtful – and this applies to most auditions really, not just for TV shows – is that you usually don't know the person sitting in front of you. On *The X Factor*, before you get to audition in front of the judges – Simon Cowell and those guys – you have to have an audition with some of the producers. They no doubt have the credentials to judge you but because you don't know them like you do *The X Factor* judges, it can feel very anonymous and at times unfair. When you get a 'No', like I had on the two previous occasions from the producers, you can be very defensive and think, *Well, who are you anyway? I don't know you, you could be a plumber!* They're not, obviously! But it does feel very harsh. However, I felt if Simon, Louis, Dannii and Cheryl were to say, 'No, Olly, you just ain't good enough', then I could honestly have accepted that and said, 'Okay, fair enough, so this isn't for me.' I was about to find out.

Just before I'd gone travelling I'd met a really nice girl and we'd gone out on a few dates and had a nice time, but it quickly became obvious she wasn't really interested in me. I was pulling out a few cheeky lines, trying my best 'cos I really fancied her, but she never kissed me or showed me any affection, so I was like, *What's the bloody point!* I decided to be all honourable and make it easy for her, so I said, 'Look, I know you've just split up with a boyfriend and aren't looking to get into another relationship straight away, I understand that. Let's just leave it there, shall we?' and she said, 'Yeah, whatever!' I was like, 'Thanks!'

Anyway she was cool, so we stopped seeing each other but when I came back from Australia we sort of started dating again, though I was kind of in a bit of a mess really. She was a great girl, she had a good job and a nice car, a house, and I just felt a bit insignificant even though I'd just been on this amazing trip. I was like, *I need to get myself back on track and a girlfriend is the last thing I need.* So I decided to cool it off, but a little while later she got in touch and said I had to go and see her because she had 'something to tell me'.

I went over to see her and she sat me down and said her mum had had a weird premonition. Now I'd heard that her mum had done this sort of thing before, but I was a bit like, *Yeah, whatever!* This girl said her mum had had a premonition that one of her daughter's friends was gonna do really well on a TV show this year, but he'd have to wear some beads on his left hand, and there'd be three things involved: a song called 'Lost' by Michael Bublé, a grey suit and a yellow tie. Then this girl said, 'I need you to wear these beads on your left wrist,' and she gave me this bracelet.

I'll be honest: I was like, 'Come on, what a load of bullshit!' She knew I wanted to do *The X Factor* again so I thought perhaps she was just mugging me off, but she seemed really genuine. I remember walking out of her house with these beads. I got in my little car and threw them on to the back seat. *Whatever!* I thought.

I drove home but what she had said stuck with me and it played on my mind for a few weeks. She kept ringing up saying, 'When are you auditioning for *The X Factor*? What day exactly? Make sure you wear the beads, Olly!'

5. Everything Changes

The day of the first audition for *The X Factor* dawned. This was to be in front of the show's production team, and if I was successful I'd get a callback in front of more senior producers. Do well there and I'd finally get to audition in front of the famous *X Factor* judges for the TV show itself.

I went to the O2 and I tell you what, it's a long day! For that first audition they request that you get there no later than 9am and if you aren't there on time, they won't see you. Without exception. The auditions go on until eleven o'clock at night, so I was sat there for hours on end and perhaps inevitably I started thinking, *Why am I doing this again? Third time, Olly! Why am I even doing this?* I kept reminding myself that the Over-25s was the category that people said was the easiest to get into (I'd just turned twenty-five). I was sort of confident that if I did a good job, I'd probably get through at least to the next round, and hopefully this year would be my year.

At one point this guy came up to me. He had previously been a contestant but was now working behind the scenes. He was being a clown and walking around trying to be the Big Bollocks, and he asked me what song I was performing for the producers, so I said, '"Mysterious Girl" by Peter Andre. Either that or "Who Let the Dogs Out?"' I was just messing with him, obviously.

Anyway, about two hours later I finally get the call and so I'm stood in front of these three producers, who ask me what I'm gonna sing. 'Paolo Nutini's "New Shoes",' I said, which is one of my favourite songs.

'Oh God! If I have to hear that one more time today I'm gonna shoot myself!' said the main producer. 'That, Kings of Leon or "Bridge Over Troubled Water". Haven't you got anything else you could sing?'

All I could think of was 'Mysterious Girl' by Peter Andre or 'Who Let The Dogs Out?'! Eventually, after a nervous pause and because of all those Motown covers I was so used to singing with F2K, I said, 'How about "Superstition" by Stevie Wonder?' He said, 'Great!' so I sang that for them. Luckily they loved it and put me through to sing one more time in front of the most senior producer, which is the audition before singing for Simon Cowell and the panel of celebrity judges. I was so excited I turned around and walked straight into the wall, which made them laugh, of course. I was just delirious with excitement!

I was so excited, I went home and told my mum and dad, and they were really happy for me, but I didn't tell anyone else, I just kept it to myself. There was still that second audition in front of the more senior producers before I'd get to sing in front of the judges. This was at the Emirates Stadium, the home ground of Arsenal. What with me being a Man United fan, I wasn't happy about going back there again! I sat in this room waiting for my name to be called out and it seemed that everyone who was going in ahead of me was getting a 'No'; it was just a constant stream of rejections.

When my turn came, I sang 'Superstition' again and Take That's 'Up All Night' in front of three producers and they liked it, so I was then asked to perform another audition, this time one that was videoed. I did that and I felt it went well, but they didn't tell me their decision that day, so I had to travel back home to Witham not knowing if I'd got through. *Finally*, after waiting for what felt like forever (it was only a couple of weeks), the phone rang one day at home and I got the news I couldn't quite believe: they had really liked my video audition too and wanted me to go and sing in front of the judges for the actual TV show.

I'd got through.

I was going to sing in front of Simon Cowell!

Obviously my family were very proud, which was great. A few days later I got the letter confirming my invitation to perform on *The X Factor*. Happy days! Once again I didn't tell anyone except close family, because I didn't want to deal with all the disappointment if I didn't do well, a hangover I suppose from the *Deal Or No Deal* experience. After all, it could all go horribly wrong and my audition might not even be shown on the telly, and then I would've looked like a complete dickhead ... again!

They tell you to wear the same outfit as your previous audition, so I had all that sorted ages in advance. I went on the internet and downloaded my maps and worked out what time I'd need to get to the ExCeL Centre in east London's Docklands. I know I'd pretty much dismissed the thought earlier, but just for luck I put on the bracelet of beads that had featured in the girl's mum's premonition. I figured, what did I have to lose? As I sat on the Tube travelling in, I knew this was one of them days that could change my life. *This could be quite special.* At the same time, it was obviously quite daunting to think I was gonna sing in front of Simon Cowell, Dannii Minogue, Cheryl Cole and Louis Walsh...

Before you sing you get given your number, then you have to do all these interviews with some researchers and then with Dermot O'Leary and Holly Willoughby (which was really exciting), as well as a chat with one of the main producers. They sit you down and you talk about your life, then they cut-and-paste the bits they find most entertaining. I said, 'I give people advice on how to save money on their energy bills. Yeah, I guess I like going out and having a good time. I mean, yeah, I suppose I am just a normal bloke, yeah, I am just a normal geezer.' When they aired the interview they played the theme tune from the TV show *Minder* which featured the famously 'slippery' car salesman Arthur Daley. I also said, 'You sing in front of the mirror and at family parties but that's really as far as it goes.'

When I watch that footage back now I think, *Where the hell did you get all that crap from?* I didn't know what I was saying! There's a lot of stuff that goes on before you even get to walk out onstage. After yet more waiting around, a group of us were called up and we started to walk towards the side of the stage area. It was quite a long way round and although the stage and audience itself were out of sight, we could hear what was going on as we waited, we could hear the auditionees singing, talking. I could hear Simon giving feedback and the crowd responding. That really ramped up the nerves, my heart was beating so fast! I was thinking, *Bloody hell, I'm going out there in a minute, Simon's gonna be there, Cheryl's gonna be there, Dannii, Louis, two thousand people, wow, this is actually gonna happen!*

I was about to find out if I could actually sing or not. I felt like I'd finally get confirmation that the likes of John down the George saying I was good enough, or the people at the gigs with the Smalltown Blaggers and F2K, were talking sense, that I did have some talent... Or I might find out I'd just been living in a fairy-tale land. If it was just nonsense, then all those gigs and all those hours spent sitting on beaches in Australia writing down my little lists, it had all been wasted, it was just a pointless dream.

My voice was going really dry. I had throat lozenges to help out but I was *so* nervous. I was trying not to think about it too much, so I was having a laugh with all the researchers, having a giggle with them, and they were all like, 'Good luck, Olly, you can do this!' They were great, really nice to me. I just wanted to go out there and give myself a good performance, to the max, play like it was my England debut at Under-21 level! My first chance to shine. If you get through to perform in front of the judges, then *The X Factor* is a once in a lifetime chance.

They film you every step of the way behind the scenes, which is quite off-putting 'cos you are trying to focus on your performance and they are like, 'How are you feeling, Olly? What's going on in your head right now?' Then they said, 'Just stand over there and go through your warm-up while we film you. You know, what you'd do before you perform...' So I'm just standing there like a right numpty pretending to dance – if you watch my audition you can see me dancing really awkwardly in a corner! When you watch that clip, you should know that I'm actually thinking, *What the hell am I doing?! Just get me out there!*

As I stood side of stage waiting to be sent on, I just tried to reassure myself with a positive mental attitude, *This is the big moment for me, this is it, this is the chance, the opportunity.*

Then they called my name and Dermot said, 'Good luck, buddy!'

Oh, crap, here it comes...

I walked out on to the stage and honestly, every step was an effort, my legs felt like jelly. I actually thought I was gonna fall over, but I just kept walking towards the X, and in my head I was going, *Oh my God! Oh my God! Oh my God!* I kept my head down for the first few steps but then I looked up and there were 2000 people staring at me, and right at the front were the judges: Simon, Cheryl, Dannii and Louis.

THIS IS ACTUALLY HAPPENING!

There were cameras pointing at me from all angles. The crowd went quiet as I reached the X and lifted my eyes to face the judges for the first time. Louis Walsh was the first to speak.

'Hello, sir.'

'Hello.'

'What's your name?'

'My name is Olly...'

Now, the TV company edit these auditions really heavily and I can tell you that my first words certainly weren't as relaxed as that sounded. I actually couldn't say my name properly at first, then I couldn't remember what my job was, but eventually I said I worked giving advice about energy bills, which got a laugh from the audience. Then Simon said, 'But you don't want to sell solar panels for a living? What's your big dream?'

For some reason I said, 'To be a pop star and be famous and sell records and be an international superstar.' God knows why I said that! I do not know for the life of me where that came from, I honestly cannot tell you. 'A pop star and be famous and sell records and be an international superstar.' Even as I said it, you can see me thinking, *Why did I even say that? What a load of bollocks!*

It's really weird when I watch that audition back; all of those words about being a pop star, selling records, and especially being an international superstar, that sounds like a confident character, like someone who knows who they are, how good their talent is ... and yet I felt none of those things. I'd have loved for all those things to happen – of course – but to be brutally honest, I didn't believe a word I was saying.

We later found out that a friend of the family was in the studio audience and he said that the vibe when I came out was that I was going to be one of the 'funny' auditions, you know, with all the stuttering over my name and job, and that as soon as I opened my mouth it was probably gonna be, 'This guy is a complete clown.' Even Cheryl told me later that she thought I was going to be a 'funny one'.

I was really *really* nervous, the most I've ever been in my life. *Woah!* Over 2000 people, celebrity judges, some of the biggest names in the country: this was certainly the biggest TV show in the country, it was really nerve-racking. At the same time, my attitude was to just go for it because the way I looked at it, if I couldn't perform in front of that many people and those judges on that day, then I was never gonna be able to do this job. This was my job interview, that was how I looked at it. If you can't sing at *The X Factor* filmed auditions, then you may as well just go home. I'd never sung in front of anywhere near that many people before; if you sing the right songs in a pub and hold a tune, people will sing along. This was a whole other level. I kept thinking, *If I'm gonna do well in this competition I have to be able to sing in front of millions on TV*, so I had to get over the nerves.

Then Simon said exactly what I had been thinking for so long, about getting my one final opportunity in front of the judges: 'Okay, well, this is your chance.'

The song started and I was just really excited to sing it. I remember singing each note like I meant it. As I sang, I just used the crowd, I didn't even look at the judges much. I was too nervous, I didn't want to make eye contact in case I could see if they were enjoying it or not. So I used the crowd, and they were my saviour. I guess I relied on my experience with my mate John in the Smalltown Blaggers, playing at all the pubs, singing with F2K, all that, and I really enjoyed it! I didn't plan how I was going to perform, I just went for it! One hundred miles an hour. All I could focus on was my own performance and making sure I gave it everything I had. It was a shot in the dark really and I rode my luck, I really did.

People ask me if I'd planned to do that little sideways shuffle (later christened the 'Olly wiggle') but I hadn't, it just spontaneously happened as I was performing, honestly. I went on instinct. I don't know why I did it, it felt good at the time, although it could have been a complete disaster, it could've come across like I was trying too hard. But I wasn't, I was just feeling the song, digging it. There's actually one point where I go too high in the song and my voice gives out, I reach breaking point, then I change back into the original key I was supposed to be in and it worked. I was relieved and delighted!

When the song finished, the crowd gave me a standing ovation and I just remember the cheers and thinking, *Bloody hell! That actually went quite well!* The judges were clapping. I was like, *This is amazing!* I knew it had gone down well because the judges had to wait for the crowd to stop cheering before they could be heard, but obviously I was very nervous to hear their comments.

Cheryl was first.

'Wow, you've got some soul in your voice, haven't you, Olly!' she said. 'Loved the moves, loved everything about it, I think you are a natural born entertainer.'

OH MY GOD!

Then it was Dannii's turn. 'You have the whole package, you are a super, *SUPER* star!'

HAPPY DAYS!

Next up, the big one, Simon Cowell.

'Olly, I've gotta tell you, I really, really like you. And, you know what, you are very, very, very cool.'

JEEE-SUS!

I just kept saying, 'Thank you.' I couldn't believe what I was hearing. He also said – but this was edited out – I commanded the stage and that it was a great performance.

Then Louis said, 'You are a natural performer! You remind me of a young Gary Barlow or Will Young, great voice, good look, the full package.' It was amazing, but it was about to get even better because when Louis asked for the vote, Simon said the words which I will never forget.

'I gotta tell you, Olly, this is the easiest "Yes" I've ever given!'

I couldn't believe what I was hearing. When he said that line I was just like, *Wow! Wow! Wow! This can't be happening, surely this must be a joke.* For any person that has done an audition, they will know that to hear that said by not just any old judge, but Simon Cowell, that was a massive moment for me.

Then the other three judges said 'Yes' too, including Dannii, who added, 'Two thousand "Yeses"' while pointing at the crowd and that was it, I was through! I walked offstage, punching the air by my side as I did, this massive wave of excitement and adrenalin taking over. Even thinking back to it now, it really makes me feel emotional.

Everything that I'd thought about before, when I'd been trudging round various jobs in factories and offices, when I'd been gigging, when I'd been in Australia, when I'd tried to convince my parents and my grandad that there was a reason to keep hoping – *I just wanna show the judges what I am all about, just one more chance* – and now it had happened.

I walked offstage from the adulation of 2000 people and I just felt this surge of energy, this amazing weight was off my shoulders. I kept thinking, *Did that actually just happen?* That audition was the single biggest compliment I've ever had, that made me who I am now, it completely kick-started my confidence … and now I was determined: *I've gotta prove these people right.*

Backstage I was treated like an absolute star. I did loads of interviews and I felt on top of the world. It really felt like the start of something, I felt like I'd just got through my first interview as a pop star, that's how I looked at it. This meant the world, it was everything. I was just walking around with a huge smile on my face. I spoke to Dermot and then they grabbed me for some extra filming for the show and also for *The Xtra Factor*.

I didn't once think that my audition was gonna actually be shown, I didn't once think this could be on TV. The exhilaration I felt was just about someone who I really respected and who knew what they were talking about telling me that I could sing and perform. For me, the judges' reaction to that audition couldn't have been more perfect, it was everything that I wanted it to be, everything I'd dreamt about for years. Finally someone in the industry – Simon Cowell! – was saying I had got a good voice and was a good performer. It was the most amazing feeling. My head was spinning. I just kept thinking, *This is the best thing that's ever happened to me!*

6. Workin' Day And Night

As much as I wanted to stick around backstage at *The X Factor* and just soak up that energy and excitement some more, eventually I had to think about going home. I headed out of the ExCeL Centre and over to the Tube and as I was walking there, I was like Gene bloody Kelly doing 'Singin' in the Rain'! Oh my days! I was jumping around, punching the air and shouting, 'Get in!' ... and strangely enough, no one gave a flying shit! Everyone around me didn't give a damn! They were – of course – just going along with their normal day but I wanted to tell the world, so I was like, *Okay, Olly, calm yourself down.* So I phoned Mum and Dad (noticing the beads still on my wrist as I did), and they couldn't believe it. I rang Nan and Grandad, then I rang my Auntie Rachel. They were all so excited for me.

After all the excitement of telling my family, I got to the Underground station and it was probably one of the weirdest moments in my life. I'd just performed in front of Simon Cowell for a massive TV show, there were over 2000 people screaming and shouting and applauding, I'd just been told it was the easiest 'Yes' Simon had ever given and that I'm off to Boot Camp, all the judges had been bigging me up, then there had been all the filming, Dermot, Holly, and yet suddenly I was standing alone on a Tube platform and ... *BANG!* Back to reality.

And it got a lot weirder too. I was sitting on a bench and some people nearby were talking and I kept overhearing the words 'Michael Jackson', then some more whispering and then, 'What about Michael Jackson?' but I couldn't hear exactly what they were saying. So I phoned a mate and said, 'What's all this about Michael Jackson?' And my mate told me: Jacko is dead.

That was just the weirdest feeling ever. Michael Jackson was a childhood hero of mine, I listened to him all the time, me and my brother used to copy all his moves, he was massive in our house. To hear about him dying on that day after everything that had happened to me at the *X Factor* auditions was just so surreal. I got home and the house was empty because Mum and Dad were away for a few days, so I put the news on and it was obviously all about Michael Jackson's death. That's the only word I can think of: 'surreal'.

I took two days off work for the audition but after that I went straight back to work, pretty much. When Mum and Dad got back, they were great, they said they couldn't believe what had happened at my *X Factor* audition. No one could really, it was a shock to everyone. Mum and Dad obviously knew I was in a band and doing lots of different bits and bobs, but they never thought that I was actually taking singing that seriously.

My success at *The X Factor* just wouldn't sink in. The rules of the show said I had to keep it a secret from all my mates and that was the hardest thing. Waiting for Boot Camp was the longest two months of my life. I was working at the time, so I had to tell work that I was going away for a week on holiday, which fortunately they were happy with, no problem.

As I headed to Boot Camp, I just kept saying to myself that I needed to keep showing the judges my entertaining side. I knew I wasn't a Whitney Houston, a George Michael or an Elton John, but I felt I could be a Robbie Williams, I could be a performer, there was room for another entertainer in this country, and I thought I could fill that gap. After those audition comments, I'd started to believe in myself, it just gave me a desire to think *I can do this!*

However, I went to Boot Camp and had an absolute *shocker*! It couldn't have gone worse. I thank God for *The X Factor* because when it was shown on TV, they'd edited me at Boot Camp as having had the most amazing week, but let me tell you this: I was awful. Shocking.

We got there on the Sunday night and I met all the other contestants in the bar and hotel. I had to share a room with some guy I didn't know, but we got chatting anyway. The first challenge was to get into a group, and I ended up with Laura White and a girl group called Belle Sorelle. I didn't really mind what song we picked, so they went with 'One' by U2.

I was tired already by the time they gave us the songs at around eleven o'clock at night but we had to be up again at four the next morning to start getting ready. The problem was I stayed up till about three learning the song! We practised and rehearsed all morning before our slot too, singing over and over and over.

Then we went onstage, the song started and *I forgot every word.*

It was horrendous. The comments from the judges were just terrible. Simon said he was really disappointed, and Cheryl said that of all the contestants she was looking forward to seeing, I had been the one she was most excited about. She'd told all her mates about me, and so now she couldn't have been more disappointed. Louis was the only glimmer of hope: he said he still thought I had talent, that he could see something in me.

They had to vote who was going through right after each performance, so I walked offstage and thought, *What a clown! What a grade-A plonker!* I couldn't believe I'd ruined my chance. I didn't deserve to go through after that.

But when it came to their decision, they put me through! I couldn't believe it. I know it was purely because of my performance at the first audition. When they put me through, I was like, *Are you serious?* I was delighted, what a let-off. It's so hard to go out at that stage and I was the only one who hadn't sung the lyrics properly. Simon didn't let me off entirely, though: he said I had to raise my game otherwise I'd be gone.

The trilby hat started to come in during Boot Camp. I'd actually worn a trilby on a few occasions previously, mostly at big summer festivals with my mates. I liked wearing trilby hats partly because of my love for ska music and bands like Madness. I was due to go to V Festival straight after Boot Camp, so beforehand I went shopping to get a few new clothes. I saw these trilby hats, so I bought a couple of them. On the first morning of Boot Camp we had to be out by six and I hadn't done my hair, so I just thought, *Sod this!*, and stuck one of these trilbies on (and yes, I still had my beads on too). The trilby quickly became my 'trademark' behind the scenes of the show, and the public picked up on it too, both during *The X* Factor and in the days since. I'd only stuck it on that first day of Boot Camp to cover up my hair but I soon began to really enjoy wearing it, so I've now got a whole collection of hats!

As a whole Boot Camp was a draining experience, horrible really, in many ways. There was so much filming that you don't see at home, and I was constantly riddled with doubt, looking around the room thinking, *What am I doing here? I've got no chance.* I was looking around the Over-25s category and it was full of talent. The one year I do it and there's talent all over the place! Every day was tough, even when we had a day off we had to watch the other people perform; one afternoon I was so tired I actually fell asleep in the auditorium. Afterwards they were filming backstage and one of the producers came over and said, 'Olly, you are nodding off in shot!' So I pushed the trilby hat over me eyes and fell asleep under that!

Boot Camp was horrible but one of the positives was meeting a beautiful girl called Laura Henderson who was in a band called Project A. I'd only really had one properly serious long-term girlfriend between the ages of nineteen and twenty-two. Funnily enough, despite everything I've said about not wanting to 'settle down' and all that, I was still very open to meeting the girl of my dreams. And with Laura, I fell big time, I cared a lot about her, really fancied her. Wow!

I chatted her up, we had a few glasses of wine, some ice creams, I sang Akon's 'Beautiful' on the guitar, serenading her – so all those lessons had worked, I guess! We snogged and all the next day I had the biggest smile on my face. I *really* liked her. That Boot Camp week was so emotional, a week of extremes, with all the stress and nerves of performing mixed in with meeting Laura, it was just crazy.

In my opinion, people don't always give the contestants on *The X Factor* enough credit because it is a vigorous process where you just don't know what's going on, you are in no-man's-land. You don't have a clue what's going on in the judges' heads, and you don't know what the public really think half the time before the live shows because the TV shows are screened way after you have done your auditions.

For the second part of Boot Camp, I'll be totally honest and admit I played it safe. We had to pick from a selection of songs and perform at Hammersmith Apollo in front of about 4000 people. I thought, *I can do this, I believe I can do this*. I chose 'Your Song' by Elton John and I didn't do badly, it was okay. I said to Dermot afterwards that I was 'really chuffed', but actually it was pretty ordinary. And once again, Simon hit the nail on the head because afterwards he leaned over to Cheryl and said, 'You know what's frustrating, here's one of those guys who could've taken a risk and instead he took the safe option. He can sing Elton John in his sleep.'

Simon was 100 per cent right. I did play it safe because that song was the only one I knew on the list and I knew I was never gonna forget the words.

If I forgot the lyrics this time I was gone, so I thought, *Just get through this audition, sing it half well, kind of perform it a bit and get through.*

They didn't tell us who was through there and then, so we had to go back to the hotel and return to see the judges the next morning. I thought, *I don't think it was my best performance, but fingers crossed.* As I walked back to the venue, I'm not ashamed to admit, the tears were going, I was struggling to keep myself together because it just meant so much to me. Boot Camp is the last step before Judges' Houses and if you get to that stage, then anything can happen. And in terms of an achievement, getting to Judges' Houses would have been amazing, even if I hadn't progressed any further after that.

They put us onstage in groups of about six or seven acts to break the news, good or bad. When they told me that I was through to Judges' Houses, well, my face said it all! It was the most incredible feeling, I just couldn't believe it. I knew I had been awful at Boot Camp. I wasn't any good, I never reached the peak of my audition, never anywhere near. But for some reason, I'd been given a chance. For me, that decision was a lifeline.

7. Welcome To The House Of Fun

After the end of Boot Camp, I saw Laura on the last night and she was leaving at half nine the next morning. I'd fell asleep on the edge of my bed the night before – I just sat back and I was gone, fast asleep in the outfit from that night! I dunno what happened but my phone alarm didn't go off and when I woke up it was half-nine the next morning! Bang on the money! I looked out of my window and it could not have been better scripted: there was Laura just coming out of the hotel reception, walking to a taxi. I ran down and got there just in time to give her my details.

After Boot Camp we just couldn't stop texting and ringing each other. She almost took my mind off *The X Factor*, this really lovely girl. For about six weeks before Judges' Houses I went to see her at her house, spent a couple of weeks there, got to know her and I really liked her. Her family were really nice too. I was so happy. Her band Project A had also got through to Judges' Houses and were going to work with Louis.

At this stage I was still working as a temp for the Energy Saving Trust, which I really enjoyed. I'd already had a week's holiday from work for Boot Camp, so when I found out I was through to Judges' Houses, I went into work and said, 'I need to have another week off, but I can't tell you why!' They said that wasn't really possible, so I had to ask for a secret meeting downstairs where I swore them to secrecy and then told them. My manager was so excited, she was brilliant, she just kept saying, 'Oh my God, you are through to Judges' Houses!' She was so supportive. Then I had to say, 'The chances are if I do get through to the Live Finals I am not coming back, but if I don't get through, then expect me back first thing on the Monday.' It was such a bizarre conversation to have!

opposite: Singing 'Superstition' for my first audition... the third and final attempt!

Just before I went to Judges' Houses, my nan loaned me some money 'cos I was skint. She lent me five hundred quid and I said, 'I will pay you back on a weekly basis. I'll earn this back, I promise,' and she turned round and said, 'Pay me back when you win *The X Factor*!'

Laura went to Judges' Houses some time before me, and we spoke on the phone, saying how amazing it would be if we were both in the Live Finals. I wanted to be with her, I really fell for her. Now it was my turn to go to Judges' Houses. I was on a plane to LA when she got the news that Project A didn't make it. I found out when I landed and I was completely gutted for her. At this point I wasn't expecting to get through Judges' Houses either, so I looked on the positive side and thought, *Well, if I don't make it through either, I've still met a lovely girl and we can make it work!*

I was delighted at making the trip to Simon's house, 'cos for any contestant that is the one thing you get most excited about, travelling somewhere exotic. I'm from a proper working-class family, with Mum and Dad always working hard and making ends meet, so there was no chance we were going to go on holiday to California; now here I was flying to Los Angeles to Simon Cowell's multimillion-dollar mansion.

My category was so strong: Treyc Cohen was an incredible singer; Nicole Lawrence was also a big voice; then there was Jamie Afro and Danyl Johnson, who had both enjoyed amazing first auditions; and also Daniel Pearce from One True Voice, who was obviously very experienced. And then little Essex boy me. Generally the other contestants were pretty cool, though I wasn't too sure on a couple of them who were a little bit arrogant: they knew they were good and they didn't expect to get a 'No'. But mostly we all got on pretty well. I felt very much the underdog, but I am a really competitive person, and I was going out there to battle.

The first day's filming started with the big reveal of Simon walking out, followed by Sinitta, who was wearing a big leaf! A great moment! Simon was the judge I wanted, of course, and now I wanted to make sure I gave it my best and got him to see more of what he'd liked so much in my first audition.

LA was amazing, what a place! Simon's house was beautiful, all contemporary design, everything was perfectly colour co-ordinated, blacks, greys, charcoals, creams, very expensive. It was stylish, stunning. We had some great trips: we all went down the Boulevard, we saw the Hollywood sign, we went shopping, it was just brilliant fun.

We got given our songs before we'd left the UK so we'd all rehearsed them loads already. I had Curiosity Killed the Cat's 'Hang On In There Baby' (which was actually a cover of a Johnny Bristol song) and also the classic 'A Song For You', which was originally written by Leon Russell but has been covered by dozens of stars over the years, including the version I was most familiar with by Donny Hathaway. Just before we performed, Simon sat us all down off camera and gave us a really big pep talk, congratulating us on getting that far but reminding us that in a way the competition was only just starting. He also said, 'Back in the UK, the show hasn't yet broadcast all of your first auditions, and I gotta tell you that one of them was one of the best I've ever seen.' After that we all sat there guessing who he was talking about, and not one person said it was me. Treyc was really nice and supportive but no one thought it was me. And in fact in the interviews before my performance you can still see my self-doubt: 'I hope that Simon believes in me...' It was all about the belief: I wanted people to believe in me. I'd lost that at Boot Camp.

My first performance was 'A Song For You' and I sang it okay, not a great performance. I'll probably never sing that song again in my life, even though it means a lot now 'cos of what it reminds me of, but I don't think it was best suited to my voice. All the time I was singing I kept thinking, *Lyrics, lyrics, lyrics*, I so wanted to make sure I didn't forget them again. I'd only got two songs to shine. I was really nervous, it was a big moment and singing in front of just two people is a nightmare for me. Now, years later, I've been lucky enough to do arena tours, so I can sing in front of 20,000 no problem, easy peasy, lemon squeezy. But even today, put me in a room with two people and ask me to sing and I will go red, get embarrassed, make bad jokes to try to ease the tension, that's just not for me. And here I was, standing in the grounds of a luxury mansion in LA, a few feet from just two people, Simon Cowell and Sinitta, both staring at me, listening to every note and syllable. Not a nice place to be. Difficult.

I felt the same after my second performance, really: they were both just okay. I walked away quite pleased, but I wasn't ecstatic, it was just a decent job. But there were five amazing singers battling against me, so I was pretty unsure of my chances. I went to bed and I lay awake pretty much all night, thinking about the next day ... thinking about decision time.

By the next morning, I was really nervous but I just kept telling myself that I'd had a great time, no one could take it away from me that I'd got to Judges' Houses, when I got back to Essex I might be able to earn a few bob out of doing a bit of TV, and I'd probably get a few gigs further afield maybe. Not once did it cross my mind that I'd get through. I was sad, though, because I'd met some great people, had an amazing time and it looked like it was all coming to an end.

We always had to get to Simon's house at midday because he liked to sleep in until noon. On the day they were announcing their decisions, they put us in that garage with his supercars that I mentioned at the start of this book. Initially I was in there with the film crews busily prepping away. The crew seemed to want me to get through, saying, 'Good luck, you deserve to get through,' stuff like that, but they wouldn't give me any indication of the decision – even though they already knew. I was the last person to go, which was really difficult.

When the crew left the garage I was all alone. I genuinely did feel like this was the biggest moment of my life. *The X Factor* is full of big moments, but to get past Judges' Houses and on to the Live Finals is huge. Then I was called up to get the news. I walked over to where Simon was sitting. It was the longest walk ever, my heart was pounding, I was nervous, sweating, thinking the worst: *How do I take this bad news?*

I remember standing there (the beads were still on my wrist!) and Simon was talking to me and he went on for so long; they only show small edited parts on TV, but Simon literally abused the hell outta me for ages! So many negatives: 'Olly, we spoke a lot about you. Let's be honest, you didn't do well yesterday, it's out of two of you who goes through.' I'm standing there, legs weak, heart thumping, thinking, *Ah, crap, that's me done for.* I was so disappointed I just lost any remaining shred of composure, but then he went into some positives, pointing out my first performance of 'Superstition' was one of the best auditions he'd ever seen, and said I was really down-to-earth and likeable ... but did he think I could sing in front of twenty million people on live TV?

Oh dear...

'Yes, I do, Olly.'

Great!

But every time I started to get excited he went into another load of negatives. It was horrendous, torture. Then he stopped and looked me straight in the eye.

That's when he said, 'You are a risk ... it is as simple as that.'

Shit, that's it, I'm going home.

'Sometimes I have to take risks. You're in.'

Those words meant the absolute world. I don't think I will ever get a feeling like that again. That single moment was it for me, that sentence from Simon at a judge's house in Los Angeles ... *BANG!* ... it took me out of that Essex life straight away. On the surface nothing had changed. Okay, I was gonna become a little bit famous on the telly, I had a chance of a pop career and I'd be singing on live TV, but after that nothing was guaranteed. However, when I heard Simon say, 'You're in,' it felt like my life changed entirely in an instant. All the doubting and worry and feeling like something was missing from life was behind me, gone; this was the start of something big for me. I was so, *so* happy.

Simon spoke to me off camera afterwards and said I'd been lucky to get through, that my first audition had weighed heavily on his decision and that I needed to raise my game. I said, 'I promise I won't let you down,' and he said, 'You better not, because I don't like to be proven wrong.'

My whole life had just changed.

8. Time To Face The Music

The flight home from LA was weird, because obviously some of the acts hadn't got through. After I landed, I went straight home and when I told the rest of my family my news (I'd phoned Mum from LA in secret), they all went mental! What a reaction! Laura was really pleased for me too, despite her own disappointment, and that was quite sad to hear her telling me how she felt. We saw each other a lot before the Live Finals started and really cemented our relationship.

About three weeks after returning from LA, I got on a train to the ITV headquarters in London and then we were taken to the *X Factor* house in Golders Green. Coincidentally, this was the same night that my very first audition performing 'Superstition' was aired on TV, so it was also the first time that people recognised me on the street; not everyone, of course, just the odd few, but that was quite shocking!

After we met up in the house, all the contestants were chatting and no one knew what was going to happen next, it was so exciting! The production team came over and told us how well we'd all done to get that far, and they warned us that we were all gonna become famous overnight, advised us to stay focused, enjoy it and respect the rules of the house, then said, 'And someone in this room is going to win *The X Factor*.'

I shared a room with Dan and Jamie. I had a great experience on the live shows, which were incredible. Before the shows themselves started, we did some photo and video shoots, and they gave us our first week's song, which for me was 'She's the One' by Robbie Williams. At this point I just wanted to get through the first week. I didn't wanna be the first to go home: that's the worst thing that can happen at this stage.

Weirdly, though, when we came to start what they call 'routining' – when you sit down with the crew and musical director to work out the arrangement

opposite: Waiting to hear my fate at the *X Factor* final, 2009

of the song and all that – I was really down. I just sat there in this room with all these really big personalities, and I just felt I couldn't do it again. *There's too many big singers, so many good people. What am I doing here?* The finalists were Rachel Adedeji, Jamie Afro, Lloyd Daniels, Jedward, Danyl Johnson, Lucie Jones, Kandy Rain, Rikki Loney, Miss Frank, Joe McElderry and Stacey Solomon. To me, they all sounded amazing, and I felt like I couldn't sing a note. I have CDs of that first routining session and you can hear the self-doubt in my voice: there's just no confidence at all. What about all that self-belief that Simon's decision at the Judges' Houses had instilled in me? It all got sucked out of me in a heartbeat. Dermot – my saviour – was brilliant: he really calmed me down and always helped when I was struggling.

Fortunately for me, my spirits quickly picked up because we all met Robbie Williams! He came in and was really chatty and incredibly helpful to everyone. I sang 'She's the One' in front of him – that's a weird thing to do! – and he was really nice about it and said he wanted to be my mate, which was a really good moment. Robbie is one of my all-time idols, he's such a great entertainer, one of the best ever in this country, so to hear that was fantastic. I got him and Simon to sign my lyric sheet for my mum and she still has that up in her hall.

When we did the soundcheck for the show, it was the first time we'd met all the judges in person, as opposed to just singing in front of them. I had my autograph book with me and I got every single one of 'em to sign it. I wasn't sure how long I'd last, after all. Cheryl said, 'Are you serious? Shut up, Olly, you're being stupid, there's no way you are going first week.' I just thought, *Well, I might and then at least I've got all their autographs.*

I was really up for it by the night of the first live show. I sang 'She's the One' and it felt really good. Every performance on *The X Factor* is the biggest one of your life. I always think it sounds so silly when other people say that but it really is. The crowd reaction was amazing but Simon said that he didn't think the song was right for me – even though he'd chosen it! Afterwards I went back to the dressing room and Simon said he thought I would get through because it was such a famous Robbie song, but that for the second week we'd have to raise my game again.

It came to the results and that was horrendous, standing there onstage, all lined up waiting for our fate. Jedward went through first – everyone loved them behind the scenes, despite the negative reaction they got from some of the public. Then Lucie was voted through ... then Lloyd ... still not me ... then Jamie ... *I'm going out, please don't go out first week ... Ricky's through, oh no, don't...*

Then I noticed that the crowd were chanting, 'Olly! Olly! Olly!' It was amazing. If you watch it on YouTube you can hear the words clearly in the background, it gets well out of hand! But still the names were called out and it wasn't mine ... 'Danyl!' ... 'Joe!' ... we were down to the last three ... *Miss Frank are through!* ... 'The final act definitely returning for next week's show is ... OLLY!' I was so pumped, I punched the air. What an adrenalin rush!

After the show, I was in the dressing room and Simon comes in and says, 'Olly, next week is Diva Week. I've got this idea, I've got a gut instinct about a song – we did it on *American Idol* a few years ago, it's "A Fool In Love", the Tina Turner classic.' So he gets his Apple laptop out and sits there next to me typing away; it was just the most bizarre thing seeing Simon Cowell putting YouTube on!

I worked hard all week on the track and it was great, I was really comfortable with the choice. But then a couple of days before the live show Simon's right-hand man said they were thinking of changing the song. I said, 'No, please don't, please tell Simon that that song is perfect for me, I've sung it loads, I'm telling you now I'm gonna smash it. I promise you!' He told Simon and the word came back that if I was happy, Simon was happy.

That choice of 'A Fool In Love' in Week Two was the turning point for me. Before then, Simon had been unsure about me, he wasn't clear what direction I should take, but with this song he found that direction: old-school retro. I was soundchecking the song one day when I could suddenly tell Simon had arrived in the room. It sounds weird but he's almost like the Queen: he walks in and everyone stops and stares! He listened to me sing this song and after he smiled and said, 'That's the perfect song choice, Olly. Brilliant.'

Don't get me wrong, I didn't speak with Simon all that much. Some of the contestants spent more time with him. Jamie and Danyl, for example, they wanted to talk to him all the time and hear what he had to say, but I felt like I didn't wanna be like that, I wanted to give him some space, he knew where I was. That said, I did feel a bit rejected, and I started wondering, *Maybe I'm not one of his favourites?* We often talked about favourites, which judge preferred which contestant, all that, but I just tried to focus and think, *As long as Simon knows I'm always working hard...*

That week's mentors were Whitney Houston and the legendary record-label boss Clive Davis. I stood in front of them and Whitney was quite reserved: she said hello but you didn't feel like you could actually go over and have a conversation with her. The week before we'd just had Robbie, who was a complete contrast, chatty and a real laugh. Whitney was more regimented, she sat down with Clive and I sang the tune but she criticised me, she didn't like it, which is fair enough, but obviously that made me feel down. Clive said a few negative things as well.

When it came to the styling for that week, they were obviously after a look that would match the old-school vibe. I expected that, but even so I was a little bit unnerved when they took out a silver suit, just like my friend's mum had predicted. I'd still got the beads on; I wore them the whole time I was on the show.

The night of the live show, Simon walked up to me and took me to one side.

'Olly, the dress rehearsal was brilliant ... but I want you to do something tonight. Before you go out, I want you to stand by the stage doors and I want you to think back to how you felt that day you came in for your very first audition, I want you to feel what we saw when you sang "Superstition", that drive, the ambition, the belief, the hunger to do well. If you get those elements right, this will be the best performance of the night. You seem a little lost and you are not believing in yourself, you are not confident enough. Get that belief back, Olly.'

During the live performance in Week Two, I knew it was going well. The crowd were going nuts and I was loving it, I was in my element. Halfway through you can see me pointing to someone in the crowd. Well, I was nodding at Clive Davis, just showing him that I was a good performer, that I did deserve to be up there, after all. I wanted to prove him wrong.

The audience reaction was just incredible and the judges loved it too. Cheryl said it was my best performance. On paper the song should never have worked, but for some reason it clicked and – as I'd promised Simon when he'd thought about changing the track – Cheryl said I smashed it.

Once again Simon had the most telling words: 'This was the person we fell in love with a few months ago during first auditions. I don't mean literally I've fallen in love with you 'cos I haven't! But it was fun, it was different, it wasn't what we saw previously, which was karaoke, it was original, and this is why all the contestants want to be mentored by me. That was really, really, really good and in a different league, fantastic!' I walked off the stage and it felt amazing, the best feeling in the world.

After Week Two that was it, I was off and running! I felt like each week I grew, Simon picked great songs for me, I started to realise what sort of artist I wanted to be – the retro old-school vibe. We did 'Twist and Shout' and 'Come Together', both by the Beatles, among many amazing songs. I stayed away from ballads, as that was never my strong point. I felt vulnerable singing slower songs because I didn't have the strongest voice technically. Joe McElderry was the big ballad singer: he nailed those. But I was still doing really well, I was getting the 'Olly chant' every week, and people even said I was favourite to win for a few weeks...

The *X Factor* house started emptying, people started to get voted off and go home. Surprisingly to me, even a few of the contestants who were getting through clearly didn't wanna be there, they didn't enjoy it or have fun, the show got too much, all the pressure and the high expectations. As soon as you do a bad performance everyone's on your case and it's very pressurised, but that's all part of the challenge. I'd say me, Joe and Stacey were the ones who loved every minute of being there, we enjoyed it, we embraced it, we had fun, we were doing amazing things, going to concerts, photo shoots, the papers wanted to talk to us, we were appearing on big TV shows, we were at events we'd never get the opportunity to go to otherwise. How could you not enjoy that?

I loved *The X Factor*, I loved being a part of it, the excitement all the way through, everything was a hundred miles an hour! Saturday nights were so exciting, we knew everyone was watching at home, having parties and BBQs, drinking and watching us on the show. I'd come off the stage each week and have hundreds of texts from my mates and family; my friend Nick was going through trains putting up 'Vote Olly' posters. It was such an exciting time. The adrenalin rush is immense – your future career is on the line every week. It's just incredible.

In the two months leading up to Christmas, we were the most talked-about people in the country, which is bonkers really when you think about it, with all the things going on in the world.

All aspects of my life were changing, the family were coming down to London, the papers were talking about me, then I got my first taste of online abuse. Sometimes people don't like you, fair enough, but when you have an

'Olly Murs Hating Club' on Facebook it's kinda odd; at least I also had a 'We Love Olly Club' too!

I also had my first taste of paps too. I was still dating Laura and I missed her a lot when I was away, so one day we'd met up and gone for a date in a local park. The next morning there was a big story with photos of us on a park bench; that was quite upsetting, and it was really weird to know that we'd been photographed like that. One of the producers came up to me that afternoon and said, 'We know you have a girlfriend but you should realise this show is about voting, and girls vote a lot. You are a popular male contestant among the fans. It's totally your decision, your call, but if you want the best possible chance of winning this show, perhaps don't see Laura as much, or rather if you still want to date her, perhaps see her more in private.' I really had to think about what they'd said and when I spoke to Laura about doing what they'd suggested, she didn't take it the best way. That was a downer...

I'd not particularly enjoyed performing in front of Whitney and Clive Davis, so I was really excited to find out who was the mentor for Week Three. I was still wearing the beads that my friend had insisted on giving me, and her mum seemed to already know what would happen next because they came in and announced that week's mentor was Michael Bublé, happy days! (He didn't sing 'Lost' but for me that was still two predictions out of two.) I'm a massive fan of Michael's, *massive*. I've got all his albums. It was Crooner's Week and they gave me 'Bewitched', which I felt was a really good chance for me to shine, a bit of dancing, so I felt very confident for once. But when I went to sing in front of Michael – who was really nice to me beforehand – he didn't like it, you could tell by his face. I couldn't believe it. I was gutted.

The performance on the Saturday went well, though, and I was voted through, but I did feel a little subdued that Michael had so obviously not liked my version. The day after the show, I was backstage and I looked up to see him walking down the corridor towards me. I assumed he wouldn't wanna talk to me, so I just kept my head down.

'Hey, Olly, Olly!' Michael was shouting after me. 'Olly, come here.' And he got my arm and said, 'Come in my dressing room.'

So now I was standing in Michael Bublé's dressing room, wondering what the hell was happening in my life! All his managers were there too, a hairstylist, a record-company guy, and Michael said, 'Everyone, this is Olly...'

I waved awkwardly and said a pretty bemused 'Hello'. It was just so weird!

'Olly, can I be honest with you?'

'Er, yeah, course...' I replied, although I wasn't sure I wanted to hear this from one of my all-time idols.

'What a great performance last night. I just don't like the song you picked. I've been asked to sing "Bewitched" a lot over the years, I just don't like the song. When you sang that song in front of me, it wasn't you I didn't like, it was the song. I was so frustrated, but man, last night you sang with so much passion! And Olly, you gotta show me how to dance!'

'Ha ha, thanks for that, that's really —'

'No, Olly, really, you gotta show me how to dance right now!'

'Er, what? In here? Now? Are you taking the piss?'

So then I had to dance in front of Michael Bublé and all these people! He was great fun, he made me laugh and we had a good old chat. Pretty surreal moment, though.

So far my friend's mum had predicted the silver suit and Michael Bublé. But what about the third part of her premonition, the yellow tie? Well, we sprinted through each week, singing, performing and wearing all different types of clothes, and one day I went in to get my clothes for that weekend's show and they styled me in this red cardigan with a white shirt and then they pulled out ... a yellow tie. I had a little chuckle to myself when I saw it but even though so far the predictions had come right and had all been in my favour, I decided not to wear the tie. I'd have looked like a bloody Redcoat! But I tell you what, there was no way those beads were coming off my wrist...

All the laughing stopped in Week Seven when I got knocked into the bottom two against John and Edward and had to sing for survival. I'd done a really unpopular performance of 'Fast Love' by George Michael. Actually I thought it was good but the audience didn't like it. John and Edward were really disliked by some people but still they were scraping through every week, so I felt pretty crap about being in the bottom two.

For my survival song, I did 'Wonderful Tonight' and I sung it from my heart for my nan, who was in the audience. I love her so much and I looked at her and she got me through it. I ended up making it through but it was a big shock to me. I realised I was becoming complacent, that's why I was in the bottom two. I needed a kick up the arse.

One person who hadn't been a part of all the *X Factor* excitement was my brother Ben. We'd begun to drift apart over a couple of years and then when I did *The X Factor* I wasn't able to tell anyone about it in those early stages of auditions. When I got through the first few rounds, I told my brother I was getting to Judges' Houses. He called me just as I was going to LA and we chatted a little bit, then he said, 'Did you ever consider me when you went for *The X Factor*?' I was like, 'What do you mean? Did I ever consider you?' He pointed out it was his wedding coming up and that if I got through to the semi-final it was the same weekend.

I didn't really think it was an issue. I told him, 'No, because we are not even at Judges' Houses and even if I get through, what's to say I'm gonna get to the semi-final?' When I came back from America, I got a phone call from Ben, he asked me what had happened and I told him I'd got through to the Live Finals, which meant it could clash with his wedding. I knew straight away that he was obviously annoyed. It ended up being the last time we spoke on the phone. That was a really tough time for me, because I sang every week and Ben wasn't there, my twin brother wasn't even around. I wanted him there more than anything.

Going back to *The X Factor*, after that shock in Week Seven when I'd landed in the bottom two I really tried to raise my game and perform with every ounce of energy I had. I worked very hard for those last weeks, rehearsed, listened to what advice was being offered, always tried to put my own spin on the individual songs, and the public seemed to like what I was doing. For the semi-final, I sang the Jackson Five's 'Can You Feel It?' and the Beatles' 'We Can Work It Out' (which Stevie Wonder also famously covered) and I got some great comments; Dannii said that not only had I got the full package but I was also grabbing it, in reference to my infamous 'Olly bulge'! Then at the end of the Results show came the news I couldn't wait to hear – I'd been voted through to *The X Factor* final.

I was in the last three.

9. At This Moment

So here I was, ten weeks in, *The X Factor* Live Final: me, Stacey Solomon and Joe McElderry. During them nine previous weeks I'd loved it, I grew as a performer, I found my niche, me and Simon got on really well, and behind the scenes I had a great time meeting some amazing people. I always felt I was the underdog behind Stacey and Joe, because they were both such great singers. Actually, though, the UK tends to get behind the underdog, so I started to think, *Maybe I've got half a chance.*

The producers told us who we were performing with and I got Robbie Williams. I was ecstatic. What a result! The build-up to the final was massive, and I just couldn't wait to get out there and perform. The whole final weekend was a massive blur. We had four or five songs to rehearse: a performance with the former finalists, a group song with Sir Paul McCartney, and our songs – mine was 'Angels' with Robbie Williams. It was a mad four days.

On the Saturday, Michael Bublé was there to sing with Stacey and he came up to me and wished me luck. There were some of his people there from Warners and one of them said they might be interested in signing me after the show had finished, but I just assumed they were being polite. I'd seen Michael signing some CDs in Week Three for the contestants but I'd not been able to get one, so now I asked him if he'd mind signing one for me. He said, 'No problem,' and went off to get one, then came back and gave me the CD case. It said, 'To Olly, lots of love. See you in the charts.'

The Live Final was so intense. After my solo performance of 'Superstition', Louis said, 'Not many people can sing Stevie Wonder ... you've definitely got the X factor, you can sing, you can dance, you're likeable, I loved it!' Simon made reference to his Judges' Houses comment by saying the decision was 'the best risk I've ever taken in my life'. Then me and Robbie did 'Angels'. People were talking about him missing his cue, but that was our fault because we changed the intro of the song. He brushed that off, though, and was amazing, saying he was 'a massive fan, he entertains me', and he even suggested that he should be taking tips off me! Then he started the Olly chant, shouting, 'Vote Olly!' What a star! After I sang 'A Fool In Love' again, they revealed the vote and I was over the moon to find out I was through to the final two.

It was Stacey that got knocked out on the Saturday, which was sad 'cos we'd got on so well throughout the show, we were best mates. There was stuff in the press about me and Stacey being together and that caused a bit of a strain on my and Laura's relationship. The speculation wasn't true, we just got on really well. Maybe my head did get turned, me and Stacey did get close but only as friends. I don't know, it was all confusing at the time. I do know that it was a shame to see her leave though.

Sunday came and it was me against Joe on the final night. Back in Golders Green at the *X Factor* house, we were in this massive gaff that had been filled with all these people, but now it was just us two rattling around in this big, empty, ten-bedroom house.

When I woke up on the morning of the last show, I just sat in my room for a while, reflecting on what an experience I'd had. I packed my suitcase and as I did I thought about all the highlights of the whole experience. Trust me, every week I got through I was so grateful, but I genuinely never once thought I was getting through. And I really wanted to experience *every* week, right through to the end. I didn't want to miss a second of the *X Factor* experience.

I wasn't thinking about the future, what might come next, I was so 'in the moment' as they say, all I could think about was doing a good performance that night in the final. I knew I'd get a manager and some gigs, get some work – wicked – but other than that I was very focused on the final night's performance.

After a performance of 'Twist and Shout', I just had one more song in my *X Factor* life. Right at the end, I walked out to sing the track that the show's winner would be releasing the following week (which previously had always gone to Number 1). This year's song was called 'The Climb', and me and Joe had already both recorded our versions so they'd be ready for commercial release. On the night, Simon wanted us to sing 'The Climb' half a semitone higher than we'd recorded it, to give it more oomph and excitement. Just before I went out to sing that track, I said to Simon, 'My voice is so sore, it's tender, I've sung too much' and he said, 'Just do the best you can do, Olly.' I went out first and you know what they say, if you are first up, then you never win the final.

It was my last-ever *X Factor* performance, and I just wanted to show my passion. I knew I had to sing with emotion, real guts, and on reflection I think I did a great job. I did struggle with a few of the higher notes, but it was a good performance. However, even as I was singing, I felt I wasn't going to win. There's a line in the song that says, 'Sometimes I'm gonna have to lose,' and I was just thinking about the emotion of the song and as I was singing I kept thinking how far I'd got to at this point: I'd worked so hard and I now kinda knew I was gonna lose the final. As I sang I was completely overwhelmed.

The judges' comments were really positive. Louis said, 'I like everything about Olly Murs, everything.' Dannii said, 'Where did that come from? ... That is a voice that we've never ever heard before,' and Cheryl loved it, saying, 'You absolutely tore that from your soul, I've never heard you sing like that Olly!' Simon was amazing: 'You just answered every criticism, when people say you are not a very good singer, just a bit of a dancer, bit of a singer, you just proved a point. I can see now how much this means to you and I really, really hope for you that people get behind you after that performance.'

Then it came to the time when you walk out with your mentor to hear the result. Even though I felt Joe was going to win, just for one split second as I stood there with Simon behind the doors there was a very weird moment, an odd sensation that I might win, after all. Simon said, 'Do you feel like we could win this too?' I did, I genuinely did, for that split second.

Dermot stood there and weirdly enough I didn't think about it being the final. I know that sounds crazy – of course, I *knew* it was the final, but I was so in the zone and so used to waiting each week to hear my name and get through to the next show. Then there was this massive surge of emotion, *Oh my God, this is the end of the show, this is it*. This journey going back to *Deal Or No Deal*, Australia, the problems with self-belief, the challenges, my grandad having a go at me at that party, me turning to my mate in Australia and saying I wanted to do *The X Factor* one more time and him laughing in my face, all these people that I had to prove wrong ... and all of a sudden my fate was in the hands of Dermot O'Leary calling out a name.

'The Winner of *The X Factor* 2009 is...'

My heart was just pumping so hard … the sensation is hard to explain.

'Joe McElderry!'

I'm not gonna lie: my instant reaction was that I was gutted, I swore (to myself), I was devastated. I really wanted to win. I looked out at my family and I could see they were all gutted too.

To be fair, Joe deserved to win. He's a great singer and a great lad, he'd been through the same experience as me and at that point vocally he was a hundred times better than me, a brilliant singer. I was the performer and I'd come second. When I spoke to Dermot I complimented Joe on his win, because he was a great guy.

Then all the contestants ran out on to the stage and congratulated Joe. Stacey come up to me while Joe was performing. I was crying and upset and she gave me a cuddle, saying some really nice, kind things to me. But I was absolutely gutted.

Straight after the show I did some interviews for *The Xtra Factor*, but it was a tough night; understandably everyone was swarming round Joe and I was sorta left on me own really. All this adulation and millions of people supporting you, the newspapers even saying you are gonna win, then all of a sudden you hear the words 'Joe McElderry!' … and no one mentions you… It's all about the winner.

I went and found my parents, they were lovely, I saw Laura, and then I bumped into Simon. He put his arm around me and said I'd done really well, which was nice, but I was just gutted. He said, 'We should sit down soon and talk about maybe signing you,' but I just took it all with a pinch of salt, thinking, *Yeah, whatever, he's just being nice. He'll be off to Barbados soon!*

I felt very negative, I was in a bit of a bad place, but I suppose I was really tired as well. Eventually I went back to the *X Factor* house, got changed out of my stage clothes and spent the night on my own there. I went to my room and thought about the whole experience. I don't mind admitting I got a bit tearful; it was a different feeling to when I'd got upset that night in the hotel after *Deal Or No Deal* – that had felt like my whole world had come crashing down – but this time I was just so gutted. You hear contestants being interviewed and they say they don't mind not winning, they are happy regardless, but as I've said, I am very competitive, I wanted to win.

The next morning Mum and Dad picked me up and drove me back to Essex, and although it was great to be back in Witham, in many ways that was the most horrible sensation, leaving the *X Factor* house in London and going back to my room at home for the first time. I just couldn't stay there, it was gonna do my nut in. It immediately brought back all the old memories of where my life had been, it felt like I suddenly went backwards.

But if you know me, you will know I don't stay down for long! After a few days licking my wounds I started feeling really positive again. I'd got a management company to look after me and my own tour manager coming to meet me. I didn't even know what a tour manager was! I'd met this guy, Mark Murphy, once before when he was looking after Brian McFadden and at that time Mark said he'd love to work with me when I'd finished the show.

I had a few days at home and it was nice to see Mum and Dad, then I got packed and ready to do some gigs. I stayed at a Travelodge with Laura the night before the *X Factor* party – don't tell me there was no glamour! – shortly after which I was due to start work. It was really nice to see her after all the emotion of the final, but unfortunately over the coming weeks I began to realise that my crazy schedule was unavoidably going to get in the way of any relationship, not just with Laura. Eventually it just became impossible and sadly I called it a day.

In that week after the final, once the party was over, a car pulled up one morning and here was this tour manager coming to pick me up to drive into London and start this next chapter of my life. Out gets this tall, bald Irish fella, he reintroduced himself as Mark … and now as I write he's my best mate.

My head was spinning when I met Mark, it really was, there was so much to take in. I just threw my bag in the back of his car and then during that journey into London, Mark just calmly explained what was going to happen. He really made sense of all the madness and uncertainty; he explained that we had loads of gigs planned, he told me how the industry worked, and he was very blunt, saying, 'You are gonna do lots of gigs, you are going to work harder than you've ever worked before, you are going to make lots of money, you will probably get signed, you will probably get a record deal, you will probably release a single …' and I was like, 'What? Really? Are you serious?'

But Mark knew what he was talking about. He'd worked with *The X Factor* before, so he knew what was going to happen next. I then met Sarah Thomas of Modest! Management. She was my new manager and she's been absolutely amazing ever since. From that day to this she's worked so incredibly hard. People don't see what goes on 'behind the scenes' and Sarah has been astounding.

Then I went to meet Richard and Harry, who run Modest!, and they were so positive and encouraging. In return, I was really straight with them, and said, 'I am a grafter, I am a worker, I don't know if I will get signed but I just want you to know that even if I don't get a deal, I am gonna work so hard this year, I will do all the gigs you want me to do, I will work my arse off.' It was such a positive meeting.

Back at home, I was looking through the post in the first week of January and there was a letter from Warners, Michael Bublé's label, saying they'd met me that time backstage at *X Factor* and they'd now like to sit down and talk to me about signing a record deal. I was like, 'Wow!' Then two weeks later, I got a call from Richard and Harry saying that Epic also wanted to sign me. Well, they work with JLS, Franz Ferdinand, Jennifer Lopez ... and of course, Michael Jackson was on Epic originally, so that just blew me away. So I went in to meet Nick Raphael and Jo Charrington there. We chatted and they said they wanted me to write down an album of tracks that I loved, so they could understand where my mind was at with regard to the music I might release. That was a great idea, so I wrote down a bit of Madness, some Stevie Wonder, some pop, all sorts of stuff.

I walked out of that meeting feeling great and as I got to the exit of the building, a car pulled up and Simon Cowell got out. He complimented me on my appearance as I'd lost a bit of weight, and we chatted a little bit – it was the first time I'd seen him since the end of the show – and then he said, 'I haven't forgotten about signing you, Olly. I want to speak to Nick and Jo at Epic about it, I want to be a part of your deal. There's something about you, I think you can do well.'

I'll be honest: I walked away from that conversation thinking he was just being nice, even though it wasn't the first time he had said it, and I totally took it with a pinch of salt. Then a few days later I got a call to say Simon had come in on the deal after all, so now I had a joint record deal with Epic and Syco, which was actually very unusual within the industry. Simon had meant every word. Result!

Not long after I'd signed the record deal, I was at a mate's house one night and the bracelet around my wrist suddenly broke, for no apparent reason, sending these little beads bouncing all over the floor. I'd worn that little bracelet all through the *X Factor* experience and every day since. I'd started to believe it had played some part in how far I'd come. I picked all the beads up, tied them together again, but they just fell apart. I tried another time, but again they fell apart, and no matter how much I fiddled with this thing, it just wouldn't go back together. Maybe its job was done? Anyway, I always keep at least one of the beads on me now, wherever I go.

In early 2010 the *X Factor* tour kicked off at various big arenas around the UK. That was a great experience, although it was slightly weird at times being with the other contestants all together again! But it was great all the same. That was the first time we got to see and perform for the real fans, and it was amazing to hear the Olly chant again! It was good to see Stacey and Joe too, they were both doing really well. There were a couple of divas on the tour, contestants who had already started changing with the fame, but overall it was amazing. I was doing my own club gigs too at the same time, and it was so exciting. Nick at Epic told me to really enjoy the tour and the club shows and have a great time because straight after we were going to start work on my debut album and it was going to get crazy busy. I was about to find out exactly how crazy that actually was...

10. Highs And Lows

Straight after the *X Factor* tour, my record label said they wanted to put me into songwriting sessions with all these big-name writers. This was just ridiculous to me, this boy from Essex. I'd never written a song in my life, I couldn't even remember the last time I'd put pen to paper and seen my own handwriting! It seemed a massive jump for me, especially when I'd realised early doors that this album would be my only shot to make a first impact. If this didn't work, I'd be finished. Looking back, it was a huge vote of confidence in my ability, to send me to these writing sessions, but at the time I was like, *The label's trusting me to go in with these famous writers and create my debut album?! Are they bonkers?*

The first sessions were with a team called the Invisible Men, so I Googled them and found out they'd written for (and with) loads of stars such as Jessie J, the Noisettes and Pixie Lott. Then for the second session I was due to write with Steve Robson and Claude Kelly, so I Googled them too and saw they'd written for Take That, James Morrison, Leona Lewis, LeAnn Rimes, Britney Spears, Akon, Whitney Houston, Jennifer Lopez... And now I'm like, *Oh, crap! I've gotta go in the studio with these guys?!*

So I was apprehensive, but I kept thinking about some advice that Robbie Williams had given me one night after *The X Factor*. He said, 'You are gonna get signed but promise me that when you get in the studio, you make sure you write the songs because they will be more personal, you will enjoy it more and that means you will create better material and people will pick up on that.'

Fortunately, the early sessions went really well, I just threw myself into it and all our efforts felt really productive. The guys at Epic laughed at me afterwards because they said that after demoing every single song I worked on, I would phone them up and say I loved every single song! It's funny, but that's how I felt, it was just so exciting to be in these studios writing songs.

opposite: Holding the official FA Cup! What an honour!

There was one reggae track called 'Feel Free', pitched by an Australian writer, that was a really great song. This was one of the first tracks that was played to me, because the label thought a modern reggae vibe would be a good direction for me. I was a bit unsure 'cos I thought it was maybe *too* reggae, but I trusted my label completely so I went and vocalled the track. That was the first time I'd done that on my own. It was crazy, down in this studio in Cornwall, a little place in the middle of nowhere with no phone signal. That first recording session was truly nerve-racking, I'm not gonna lie, because vocally it was all very new. I didn't know what range I could hit, what key I could do, anything really … but I sung it, I gave it everything and it was really fun.

Then we did some more writing sessions and I came across the start of a song called 'Love Shine Down'. I wrote some more on to that and started to really get into the process. The funny thing is, it wasn't until much later that I found out that it was actually Ed Sheeran who'd started writing that song! And even more weirdly, I then found out that some of the original backing vocals were by Jessie J, when she was still a session singer!

Eventually we'd written about forty songs and yes, I loved almost every single one of them. We needed the all-important debut single but it was really hard to choose because it was just so crucial. Pick the wrong song and it could all be over before it had started. We had a tune called 'Hold On' that used a Bugsy Malone sample and the label were initially all up for that to be the debut single; that Australian writer's tune, 'Feel Free', was still popular too, but I just felt that if we could somehow find a combination of both those songs, then we'd have the ideal single. That's what 'Please Don't Let Me Go' seemed to be when we first wrote it, and sure enough, it turned out to be my very first single.

'Please Don't Let Me Go' was summery, it captured my personality and felt really good. I vocalled it, then we got it produced by Future Cut and when it came back we were all like, 'Yes!' Nick and Jo at the label were so enthusiastic about it. A few doubters said it wasn't a hit but these two had no doubts, they said it would be massive, they even took wagers!

Oddly enough, while this was all happening behind the scenes, as exciting as it was, I felt a little bit like my public profile was slipping. I wasn't on TV, I wasn't touring, people weren't tweeting me as much as they had before, not many people were saying hello in the street, it just seemed to be fading. It was a weird time of contrasts. Maybe it wasn't going to work out, after all?

While I was waiting to release my first single in August 2010, I got a phone call from Robbie Williams, something which still felt rather bizarre! He said, 'Olly, I'm doing this big charity football game again. It's called Soccer Aid, it's a huge event, we will play at either Old Trafford or Wembley in front of 75,000, there'll be loads of celebrities, it's gonna be shown live on ITV1, looks like we have Giggs and Zidane playing. Are you interested?' and I was like, 'Are you having a laugh? A hundred per cent, I'm in!'

The day came to arrive at the Soccer Aid hotel and I was well up for it. When we all met up for our briefing, I noticed a few of the celebrities involved weren't particularly welcoming towards me, and I definitely got that vibe that they thought, *Who's this guy? Some bloke off* The X Factor?, which wasn't a nice feeling. Robbie was the complete opposite, he's never treated me with anything other than total respect. I was telling him about all these writing sessions and he said, 'Great! Go to your room and get your laptop, Olly, I wanna hear these songs!'

So a few minutes later I found myself in the very bizarre position of sitting in Robbie Williams's penthouse suite, playing him all these tunes I'd written, on my laptop. This massive idol of mine wanted to hear my songs. I played him 'Please Don't Let Me Go' and he loved it, giving me some great feedback... But I can't deny it was really strange!

Soccer Aid was brilliant. We raised loads of money and the whole event was a massive success. On a personal level, obviously I loved playing football with so many legends and famous faces, and afterwards I noticed that people seemed to view me in a different light, lads especially. I think that match was a turning point in many ways. Soccer Aid has since become an annual extravaganza and I was fortunate enough to be asked to play again in 2012, which was great, even though I had to come off early with an injury. What is it with me and footballing injuries, eh?

Back in the summer of 2009, it was just one first-time experience after another. I was learning so much stuff literally every time I walked out of my door. With 'Please Don't Let Me Go' lined up for release in August, we had to film my first-ever video. The footage was shot at this beautiful home in Reading, with loads of dancers from *The X Factor* as it happened, so it was nice to see them again. The idea was centred around a house party with me trying to find this beautiful girl. To this day it's the longest shoot I've ever done, which was a bit of a shock to the system, but the end result was amazing. I was so chuffed.

Another *first* came when I was in London traffic one day and 'Please Don't Let Me Go' came on the radio; it was the first time I'd heard my song on air. What a great feeling! I felt like leaning out of the car window and telling everybody, 'Listen! That's me, that's my song!'

By now, the reaction to the single was really positive, and my belief in myself was getting stronger all the time. I worked really hard in the lead-up to, and during the week of, release, doing radio promo, magazine interviews, TV – it was manic. Katy Perry was releasing 'Teenage Dream' the same week so I thought there was no way I could get a Number 1 now! But we had such good momentum, fantastic radio support, around a million YouTube views in five weeks, and a huge reaction from papers, magazines, Twitter and Facebook, I just had a funny feeling that my fans were gonna do us proud.

I did one interview with *Heat* and they asked me what I would I do if I did get to Number 1 after all. I don't know why I said it, but my reply was, 'I will get naked!' They thought I was just joking, so I said, 'I mean it, in fact I will get naked for your magazine! Trust me!' It's not like I'm even confident with my top off either! Sarah was with me that day and she said, 'Olly, what did you say that for?!'

That period of huge excitement was also a very difficult time for me privately. It was around the release of my debut single that my brother sold a story to a newspaper. I was at V Festival on Saturday and we'd had a tip-off that one of the papers was going to run a story. Me and Sarah thought, *I'm sure it'll just be a small piece somewhere...* Unfortunately the paper put it on the front page, with the headline 'Olly has wrecked our lives'.

I'd like to think that my brother was a bit naïve and that he went into it thinking it was just a small piece too. But whatever the reasons behind it, the release of my debut single was one of the biggest – and happiest - moments of my life. Everything I'd done in the past year was leading up to this moment.

I just wanted to talk about my single but for the press, this was a big story so every interview I did about my single became about my brother. I asked the former TV presenter Andi Peters – now a top media trainer - to help me get around what to say. I'm not a horrible person, I'd never be horrible to anyone, so I didn't want to make things worse by talking about it. I still don't like talking about it now, after all *he's my brother*. I love him, I'm always gonna love him, but that doesn't mean I'm gonna like him for what happened.

It's such a shame this all had to happen because as a family we are close. My family are really important to me.

I don't think that we will ever have the same relationship again, I don't think that we will ever be the same as we were for the first twenty-five years of our lives. I think we are changed now, we are different men. I've moved on and he's moved on. But I always say – and I firmly believe this – that time is a healer. I believe that in years to come things could change and I am sure they will. I am sure he will be sat around the living room with my mum and dad again at some point.

11. Thinking Of Her

Away from all the upset with my brother, my life was just getting crazy! The week of the debut single's release was a strange, exciting, mad time. I even had a documentary crew following me round for ITV. I really wanted to get the Number 1; I'd been on the chart-topping *X Factor* single, of course, but that was not my own record, this was totally different. We were getting the single's sales figures through each day and at first Katy Perry was in front, then she fell back again and I was ahead but although in the midweek listings we were Number 1, towards the weekend she was outselling us again.

Then I got a phone call.

'Olly, you've been booked to go into Radio 1 on Sunday 'cos potentially you might be needed on Reggie Yates's Top 40 show...'

'Yes! Happy days!'

'Hang on, Olly! They also have guests that only get to Number 2 or 3 as well!'

'Oh, crap.'

On the Sunday morning, I was at home with Mum and Dad sitting at the table anxiously waiting for the call. I was still being filmed by the camera crew so they were with me the whole time. After what seemed like an absolute age, the phone rang – finally! – and it was Nick from the label.

'Olly, you want to know, don't you?'

I told him I thought we were Number 1. As I sat there in the half-second waiting for Nick's answer, a million thoughts shot across my mind. Getting that Number 1 would be such a massive relief, and as I waited for the news the adrenalin surging through my body was huge. If I was Number 1 I'd be ecstatic, on top of the world. We'd all worked so hard, the travelling, the radio tour, the interviews, the PR was huge, we all deserved it. But what if I wasn't...?

opposite: In front of my home crowd in Chelmsford, Essex – summer show 2011

Then Nick said, 'We are there by 7000 copies.'

We were Number 1! Get in!

Afterwards I went back on the phone to Nick and he said, 'Oh, Olly, there is some bad news, though...'

'Oh God, what now?'

'You've got to get naked!'

We quickly started promoting the second single due for release in November; it was called 'Thinking of Me'. We did another video with all the shots of me perched on top of those railings, defying gravity in a really sharp suit! I managed to slip in a few of my ska influences too with the thin braces and button-up shirt. The real highlight of that single campaign was performing the song on *The X Factor*. That was really weird, going back to the show, seeing all the surroundings, the production staff, the judges' chairs, backstage, and being around all the emotions of the contestants. The week before we had all these discussions with Simon because he wanted to make the song more Christmassy! Eventually we came to a middle ground that everyone was happy with and so by the night of the show I was pumped, I really wanted to prove a point.

By now the new series of *The X Factor* had really kicked in and there was all this new talent coming through, like One Direction, Cher Lloyd, Matt Cardle and Rebecca Ferguson, so I wanted to show how good I was. I wasn't nervous at all, I couldn't wait to get out there and do my thing. I mingled with the contestants loads, everyone was happy, there was a real buzz around the studio. We did the soundcheck and a couple of the One Direction boys watched it and really liked it.

My debut album was due out a week later too so it was a big performance. When Dermot introduced me, it was fantastic to hear him say, 'He made it all the way to the final, he's already had a huge Number 1 hit ... and we are so proud to welcome back ... Mr Olly Murs!' Then they ran this VT, which was really emotional to watch, showing all my best bits from the show and since. By the time the song started, I was almost too excited! Sometimes I have to calm myself down on stage.

We performed 'Thinking of Me' with this amazing production, a big routine with loads of dancing, and I changed one of the lyrics to 'I bumped into Cheryl down in Waterloo'. I was always a big fan of hers, always fancied her, but I could never talk to her, 'cos she's just amazing. So anyway I did the performance and Simon spoke to me, then Dermot came over too, and they were both so complimentary. Cheryl was waiting behind Simon and after he moved off she came up to me, and I was like, *Oh my God, this is totally surreal.*

I was standing there pretty much just staring at her, thinking, *She is so gorgeous!*

'Olly, that was brilliant, I really enjoyed it...'

'Thank you, Cheryl,' I replied, while actually thinking, *Jesus, you are so good-looking.*

'It was really confident, looked like a lot of fun,' she said.

'Yes, it was fun.' *Perhaps I should try to get her number?*

'Have you been all right then, Olly?'

'Yes, thanks ... er ... yup, great.' *Or perhaps I should offer her my number?*

I couldn't actually think of anything else to say. I'd got nothing else to say! There was a bit of an awkward silence.

'Er, yeah, I've gotta go now, Cheryl, okay...'

'Yeah, okay, see you then, Olly. Good luck with everything!'

'Thanks.' *Oh my God, she's so good-looking...*

After the show, my Twitter went nuts, everyone was texting me. It was a fabulous night. I went out with the JLS boys to celebrate and somehow lost my wallet. Bizarrely, the Irish international footballer Robbie Keane found it on the street and handed it in! So even though I didn't get Cheryl's number, I guess it was my night in the end.

12. A Chance To Shine

My debut album, *Olly Murs*, came out in November 2010. I was really proud of the record because, after all, it was my first chance to write and show people what I could do with my own music. There was a reggae vibe throughout and the record came together relatively easy, as we had some really strong songs. We did discuss various other titles for the album but in the end we thought that self-titled was best: it was my introduction to people, so it was best that I keep it simple. I'm proud to say that I think it was a great pop record.

Just like the first single against Katy Perry, my album had some stiff competition, in particular from the new Take That record. But my album just flew off the shelves, and even though it didn't get to Number 1 (stalling one place behind), I'd secured the biggest opening-week sales for a debut act in the whole year. The record sold 300,000 copies in the first three weeks and went platinum before Christmas (it eventually stayed in the charts for over a year). The act that stopped me from getting to Number 1 was – of course – Take That, so no shame there. I got an email from Robbie that weekend and he said he was well proud of me but apologised for his band deciding to release an album against me!

Christmas 2010 was really special. I bought my family some amazing presents. I'd already long since paid my nan back the five hundred quid I owed her because Grandad kept mentioning it and you now know that he doesn't exactly mince his words! So now I paid for them both to go with Mum and Dad to Vegas and Graceland, which I'd said I'd do all those years ago if I won some money on *Deal Or No Deal*. My sister's present was slightly less glamorous: she got a boiler in her house! There was an extra buzz that year too because my sister announced on Christmas Day that she was pregnant. We were all so excited for her and her husband Ben.

opposite: With Team Olly holding up magazines with my first ever front cover!

OLLY MURS: HAPPY DAYS

No doubt about it, 2010 was an incredible year. At the New Year's Eve party at home, we actually played my whole album, it was so embarrassing but it was also really nice in a weird way. And if you should judge a year by what you achieved, then I was pretty proud of those twelve months' efforts.

Sometimes your success catches you off guard. You have months go by when you don't reflect on whether you have done well or not, usually because you are just so busy working that you don't give it a second thought. When you do try to look back you're usually still too hectic anyway, so it's hard to really step out of the madness and see what's happened. But other times, life has a way of reminding you.

Just before Christmas of 2010 I had a car accident. I was driving round to my mate Jeff Brazier's for lunch in Harlow and it was really snowy and icy. I was in my little *Inbetweeners* car, an old red Fiat Cinquecento which cost me £825. That car had become a bit of a trademark with the local lads, who were always taking the piss out of me. I once got a speeding ticket in it and I was fuming. I wouldn't have minded but that car barely went over 40mph! Anyway, on this particular really cold day, I drove round a corner and hit this patch of black ice. So I've skidded and gone straight into the central reservation, ripped all me car open, and clipped this other guy's car in the process.

Bless him, the guy came over to see if I was all right. My Fiat was blocking the road, so me and this geezer pretty much picked it up and moved it, just the two of us. That's how lightweight that car was! Then we went over to his car to get his details – and this is the God's honest truth – 'Thinking Of Me' was playing on the radio! The guy looked at me and just burst out laughing!

I took his details and went back to sit in my car, waiting for Dad to come and pick me up. It was freezing, so I put the heater on full blast in this half-mangled car, feeling shaken up and cold, wondering what had just happened, still chuckling with a smile about my song being on that guy's radio. As I sat there in the icy car, the windows frosting over, there was a knock on the window. I wound it down with my freezing cold fingers and there's this woman standing there with her kids, asking for a photo.

Going into 2011, I had a theatre tour booked for the spring, so I had a lot of rehearsals and planning to get through. I figured it would be a good idea if

I went away for a break first before it all kicked off. I went into Colchester with a few of my mates and we walked into a travel agents' and asked about holidays where we could find a few clubs, nothing too lairy, some good pubs, somewhere busy but not mad. The girl behind the counter sold me a week in Malia! Anyone who has ever been to that part of Crete will know this is pretty much your typical 18–30-type destination! Real rowdy. In retrospect, it was probably the very worst type of place to go on holiday with my mates just after getting a Number 1, but I was about to find that out the hard way.

I'd been for a stag weekend in Ibiza just beforehand and that was all fine, the documentary film crew were still with me and it was good fun. But Malia would prove to be very different. It started well – the hotel was very glamorous, although it seemed to be mainly full of old people. That didn't bother me, but some of the lads were like, 'Where's all the birds?'

They didn't have long to wait! On the first night we went out it was manic, and I knew immediately that I'd made a mistake. I thought, *I've had an absolute Weston-super-Mare here*, but my mates were loving it. All these gorgeous girls were coming up to me, and my mates were like, 'This is the best night ever!' However, by about one in the morning it got really rowdy, guys started shouting things at me, I was getting abuse, it quickly became very uncomfortable. I felt very vulnerable even though I was with my mates, and in fact it was the first time I'd felt that vulnerable in public. There was no tour manager around me, no security, and all of a sudden I'm in a club with girls coming up to me and blokes swearing at me. Before I booked the holiday, I hadn't given any of this a second thought. Why would I?

The atmosphere got worse after only a couple of days. I heard about some guy on the island slagging me off online and one night after I'd had a few drinks and got agitated, I went and found him and we had some strong words. I actually felt bad afterwards but I did need to show people that you can't just say that stuff and not expect to piss me off. After that my blood was boiling.

Another night I went into the toilet in this bar and I walked past these two geezers at the urinals who said, 'All right, Olly!' I said, 'Hi' back and went in the cubicle and shut the door. But as soon as I turned the lock, these two guys started slagging me off, saying all these horrible things about me and swearing at me. They were spitting their words out so viciously, they clearly didn't want me on the island. When I came out of the cubicle, they shut up and were like, 'All right, Olly, how's it going?' It was the first time I'd had that experience and I found it very unpleasant.

I walked out of that club really angry and headed up the strip, saw another club I wanted to get into but I had words with a guy there too and then I just completely lost it. My mates grabbed me and calmed me down, but not before it had been captured on CCTV. The next day the *Sun* ran a piece called 'Olly's off his trolley', with grainy black and white snapshots of me being held back by my mate outside this bar.

There were other stories in the newspapers too, about girls and other stuff. It was all ridiculous, but after that week away it really hit home that whether I liked it or not, my life had changed, it wasn't the same. That holiday was mental – wrong place, wrong time, wrong everything – but in retrospect it was the best thing that could've happened to me because I realised that when you come into the public eye even slightly, there are certain situations you cannot put yourself into any more. Back then I didn't know that. I was, and still am, one of the lads, the boy from Essex who's done well, but at that point I just thought, *So what if I've had a song out? I can still go on holiday with my mates, no one's gonna ask for a picture, no one's gonna give two craps about me in the corner of some club.*

When I got back from Malia and thought about what had happened, I was even more agitated, because now I felt very isolated. What did this mean? No more lads' holidays? I don't want to only go out if I get VIP treatment, that's not me. What I later learnt was that you just need to pick your destinations with more care. Don't go to Malia on the piss, for starters! But seriously, I took another holiday shortly after in Barbados which was much quieter, everyone was lovely. I went with a mate, James, but there was hardly any bother. Another lesson learnt.

As it turned out, Barbados was memorable for an entirely different reason too! We were out one night at a bar and bumped into Eliza Doolittle, which was weird in itself, and we all went for an Italian. We were chatting away, then all of a sudden I heard this really familiar Canadian accent.

'Oh my God, Olly Murs.'

I looked round and Michael Bublé was standing there; he'd just walked in with his family.

'Oh my God, Olly, I was just talking about you when we were on the beach today. This is freaking me out. Oh my God, your album is killing it, dude!' He was saying all these amazing things, being so nice to me. I looked across at my mate James – who was sitting next to Eliza Doolittle and looking up at Michael Bublé talking to me – and his eyes were just wide open, he was in a daze.

We chatted for a few minutes and then Michael and his family sat at a nearby table. He got them all sat down and then I could hear him still talking about me, but he was only about ten feet away so we could hear every word.

'Basically that guy over there is Olly Murs. This guy is an amazing performer, he's got everything, he was on *The X Factor...*'

I was like, 'Michael, I can hear you! Stop saying nice things,' and he was ribbing me and there was all this banter. He was so kind to acknowledge me, to say hello the way he did and pay such respects. I was like, 'Wow, wow, wow.' Ever since then we've kept in touch and he's been a great friend.

And no, I'm not going back to Malia.

13. Perspective

In January 2011 I got a phone call from someone at Comic Relief saying they wanted me to do a desert trek in Kenya for that year's fund-raising campaign. Two years prior to this, Gary Barlow and eight other celebrities, including Cheryl Cole, Chris Moyles and Ronan Keating, had climbed to the top of Mount Kilimanjaro, so Comic Relief wanted to do something similar again. The plan was for a bunch of celebrities to trek through the Kaisut desert on a jaunt of around seventy miles, in 40-degree heat.

I was so thrilled to be asked. What a privilege! I had 'Heart On My Sleeve' due out as a single in March and 'Busy' was due to be released shortly after, so I was really hectic, but in a heartbeat this was my priority and I didn't for one second hesitate in saying 'Yes'.

The second we hit the runway in Nairobi it was such a culture shock. I'd travelled to Australia and Egypt but other than that I hadn't really travelled that much. This was a way of life I had never experienced before, so it was a real shock. The poverty was unbelievable, from the minute we came out of the airport. We got in a car and started the drive to the hotel and in minutes we were passing all these slums along the side of the road. There were kids wandering around, scavenging for food, just so completely vulnerable, it was such an eye-opener. At one point we stopped for a break near this particularly bad slum and there were all these kids running up to us asking for food or clothes, and trying to sell us stuff. I just wanted to give them everything I had, it was awful. Then I noticed a massive billboard advertising a flat-screen 3D TV, literally right next to this slum. I remember thinking, *How many people around here can afford a telly? Most of them haven't even got a house!* It was just a very sad juxtaposition.

The trip's aim was to raise awareness of, and funds for, the amazing work they do to combat trachoma and cataracts in these underdeveloped

opposite: Playing games with the kids in Kenya!

countries. So the film crew took us to a local hospital where they were treating huge numbers of Kenyans who were turning blind as a result of their diseases being left untreated. I met one patient, this fantastic guy in his sixties, who sat with me and explained how his cataracts were so bad that he couldn't work and therefore couldn't look after his family; he was the breadwinner but now he couldn't see.

We chatted for a while and then he went for this operation, and after he left to get treated I felt really down and upset. I just kept thinking, *What if it doesn't work? Imagine if he can't see his kids again?* I'm not particularly religious but I was sitting there, thinking, *If you are up there, God, please give this guy his sight back.* Not every operation worked, you see. Anyway, I was delighted to find out that the operation had worked and he got his sight back. What an incredible day, from the depths of despair to such joy for this guy. They were just giving people *hope.*

Following the hospital trip, all the guys turned up for the trek and we met all the helpers. After seeing the slums and then the work at the hospital, I was now so driven to get on the trek, finish the walk and raise the money. Alongside me were Dermot O'Leary, Lorraine Kelly, Radio 1 DJ Scott Mills, the actresses Kara Tointon and Ronni Ancona, singer Craig David, presenter Nadia Sawalha and the quite amazing blind presenter and broadcaster Peter White. There was a great team round us too, with some SAS guys to help out, as well as local guides who really knew the terrain and the real dangers of the hostile environment, the dangerous animals and all that.

I know people watch these shows and say, 'I bet they are sleeping in caravans and having pizza and beer delivered every night...' but I can tell you now, we proper, PROPER did this trek. Every day we walked miles in blistering heat: I think the longest single walk was over twelve miles and the temperature rarely dipped below 40 degrees. We had an interpreter with us who spoke to the various tribes we met along the way, reassuring them that we weren't there to harm them or steal their cattle, and it was amazing to see.

At the end of each day we set up camp but we were all worried sleeping in these tents, because we'd heard all these stories about hyenas, lions, African wild dogs and all these deadly creatures scurrying around. I remember one particular night we got to the end of the day's walk and the camp setting looked exactly like something out of *The Lion King*. I was waiting for Scar to jump out of his lair with all his hungry hyenas. So I said to one of the guides, 'Is this safe here? Like, could a lion be hiding here?' and he said, 'Oh yes, but remember, Olly, the lions, they are everywhere.'

'Oh, that's okay then!'

There was some seriously good banter among the gang, even though it was a very hard experience. The crew and guides cooked us some great food, but there was loads of goat meat, which is pretty chewy! One night I was sharing a tent with Craig David and we spotted this scorpion in with us and totally crapped ourselves. Craig started throwing hot water on it and we were chucking things at it, going mental, acting like a couple of wusses inside this tent. In our defence, we'd been told that if one of these things stings you, you ain't trekking any more, you are on a plane to hospital because you might lose your leg. Now, Craig is a big guy, and I'm a lad too, but we were just jumping about making a total hash of it. It took us about twenty-five minutes to kill this thing.

After we'd recovered our composure, we went over for dinner and as we were sitting down, this guide went to get something out of a nearby jeep, and as he lifted the boot Dermot spotted another scorpion in the vehicle. He shouted at the guide to watch out, the guy saw the scorpion, then in an instant lifted his leg really high in the air and brought it down like an axe on the creature, killing it instantly. It was like a scene from *Mortal Kombat*, a trained killer at work. We just fell about laughing. What a difference to the way Craig and I had flapped about trying to kill the one in our tent earlier! We laughed even more when we realised this guide was just wearing flip-flops.

They were constantly warning us about our hygiene, and we had to use anti-bacterial liquid and wash our hands all the time, because there was just so much bacteria around and getting diarrhoea could be very serious in that intense heat. Anyway, to cut a long story short, on the night before the last day of the trek, I knew something was up with my stomach, and I slept really badly because it was so painful. By the middle of the night, I suddenly had to jump up and run to the makeshift toilet.

This 'toilet' was actually just some pieces of wood perched over a hole in the sand, into which we all did our business. I made it there in time, and in the wave of relief that followed I tried not to shout 'Aaaaahhhhhhhhh!' too loud and wake anyone. As I did, I looked up and it was the first time in my life I'd seen a sky like that, the darkest blue, with millions of these sparkling, bright stars shining down. It was the most beautiful thing I'd ever seen. The moonlight and stars were so bright I didn't really need my lamp any more. I sat there for about five minutes, chilling, just soaking up this incredible view.

Then, not to put too fine a point on it, it was time to wipe my bum. I leant down to get the toilet paper off the floor and it was then that I suddenly noticed the floor was moving. I looked again and realised to my horror that it was covered with thousands of insects, bugs, scorpions, ants, everything! This time I didn't worry about how loud I shouted, though now it was 'Arrrggghhh!' instead, and I wiped my arse in record time, yanked my trousers up and ran to my tent as fast as I could.

The next day was the last but there was no sense of relief for me, I was just in too much pain. I trudged the last ten miles with this horrendous stomach pain, and every five minutes I'd have to crawl behind some bush and pull my pants down. The medics made me take these really strong tablets for dehydration, so I was woozy and in pain, it was horrendous. It was a really horrible day but all of that pain and discomfort vanished in a second when I could see the finish line where all these kids and locals were waiting for us. From being one of the most painful days of my life, it was instantly one of the best, a real sense of achievement. I was crying for all of that last mile.

The whole trek experience was just overwhelming, such a privilege. We raised a lot of money and hopefully helped a lot of people. From a personal point of view, that trip for Comic Relief was perfect timing because it put everything into perspective – *very quickly*. I'd just had my debut album doing so well, been to Barbados chatting with Michael Bublé in a restaurant, new singles, a tour, I was looking forward to all the exciting plans we had for 2011... You can so easily get carried away in this industry. Fame, money, cars, big houses, all that: you can soon get lulled into that lifestyle and lose your sense of perspective.

So to then walk into a way of life where everything is so different and such a massive culture shock, it really made me realise how lucky I am. In fact how lucky we all are. There were parents out there who didn't know where the next meal was coming from, parents who were watching their kids die from illness, and knowing that even if they did recover, there was a pretty good chance their children wouldn't live as long as they had.

You can't ever forget how lucky you are. I've done a few charity projects and I get a real buzz out of being able to help in some small way. I went back on a celebrity edition of *Deal Or No Deal* but that show must have it in for me because this time I only won 50p!; I did 'Let's Dance for Sport Relief' with Scott Mills, which was great fun; and I've done a celebrity 'Mother's Day' special of *Who Wants To Be A Millionaire?,* which was great fun sitting alongside Mum, and we got to win £10,000 for our chosen children's charity, Brainwave. I've even since become a patron to Brainwave. They are an amazing little charity with a centre just down the road from me in Witham. They do great work there, and it's a perk of the job to be able to raise awareness and money for important charities like these.

Things could've been so different for me. I could have been born in Kenya. Any of us could. That trek through the desert made me determined never to forget that.

14. You Shine So Bright ... But I Can See You're Not Yourself

After we came back from Kenya, I released 'Heart On My Sleeve', which got to Number 20 (not bad considering the album had been out ages!). That was great, then it was time to head out on my first-ever headline theatre tour, but before I did I worked on Radio 1 with Chris Moyles for a week, and that was a lot of fun too. My life was constantly busy, long hours all the time, but I was loving every second. People often ask me why I haven't got a girlfriend in my life, and I say I probably would have if I didn't have such a busy schedule! Look what happened with Laura, she was a lovely girl and we had a great time but it became impossible to keep the relationship going. Right now, working is my priority and I love it so much.

Some of the press have questioned that and I've also had my share of criticism for other reasons, and sometimes it can get very personal and hurtful. You kinda wonder why they get so vicious, but after a while I realised that there's no point worrying about it, because at the end of the day my fans enjoy what I do and for as long as they want to hear me sing and watch me perform I will continue to do this. They are the reason why I am doing this. After all, I wouldn't be sat here now if wasn't for those people who voted for me on *The X Factor*.

I know I'm not everyone's cup of tea, but for my fans, those people out there who spend their hard-earned money on my records and concert tickets, and support me so amazingly, I am *their* cup of tea.

Seeing all of those people who had supported me so incredibly on that very first solo theatre tour was an amazing experience. Those shows were

opposite: On stage at Wembley Arena at my first arena tour 2012!

everything I ever wanted, thirty-six dates sold out, all on my own. We'd assembled a great band who were all very seasoned, but it was all new to me: ten days of intense rehearsals, putting the set together, getting the show just right, getting on my own tour bus for the first time – it was all so exciting.

The first night was in Rhyl but I wasn't particularly nervous, I just wanted to get out there and perform. The only thing I was ever worried about was my voice, 'cos I'd never sung this much before. I was used to maybe forty-minute sets but even then sometimes my voice would be tired and sore. Now I'd gotta do an hour and twenty minutes; there weren't many days off either, so for example we did three consecutive nights at Hammersmith Apollo, and that was a real challenge for my voice.

This was all part of the learning experience I was on. The voice is a muscle, which I didn't know before I started singing professionally. There are singers who are just amazing even from a very young age, totally natural, but I only really started singing at twenty-three in pubs. I had to quickly learn about tuning – am I in key? – my breathing, controlling my stomach muscles, my diaphragm, my throat... I was learning all the time. On that first tour I really worked hard at it, though I did struggle on some nights, which was frustrating 'cos I wanted every show to be brilliant, but I really tested and pushed myself and as a result I think I grew as an artist.

Among all the 'firsts' I was experiencing, it was also the first time I'd seen my fans properly, up close, at one of my own shows. I'd done a lot of gigs up and down the country, my album was double platinum, I'd had four singles out – two charted in the Top 5, one went to Number 1 – so I knew there were fans out there, but it was amazing to see just how many and even better to be able to perform and talk to them so intimately. It was also great to travel up and down the country on tour to loads of different cities and towns – I absolutely loved being on the road.

There was a great vibe on tour, every night we gave it everything, but then really quickly it was all coming to an end. Not that I was going to get any time off – JLS had asked me to jump on board their summer tour, so I had two days at home then it was off on the road again! Those JLS dates were enjoyable, although it did rain almost every show. It was very interesting – and motivating – to see the hype around the JLS boys, how well they've done. I got to witness first-hand their drive and ambition and how hard they work. They are great guys. It made me want to play my own stadium shows even more.

Towards the end of my theatre tour, I was up in Scotland when Richard Griffiths from Modest! Management called me. It had previously been mentioned that the spin-off programme *The Xtra Factor* might be interested in me presenting the show, and Richard was phoning to say that they had actually now made me a formal offer. My initial reaction was to say no, as I was worried that even though I felt I could do the job they wanted me to do, my music career was going so well and going on TV presenting and trying to be a singer at the same time probably wasn't gonna work, it was too risky.

Richard said to think about it for a few days, so I came off the phone and spoke to Sarah, my mates and my family. Then I spoke to Nick at Epic, who is a very enthusiastic character and sees the bigger picture, and he said some things that made so much sense. He really felt it was a great opportunity for me.

I came off the phone from Nick and my whole view had changed. After that I spoke to my tour manager Mark too. We talked it through for about two hours and I finally came to a decision … I said 'Yes' to presenting the show. Now 2011 was about to get even more crazy!

We pretty much went straight into auditions for *The Xtra Factor*, and bless Sarah, she did loads of travelling with me auditioning with the show, then travelling on days off to meet up with songwriters for work on the next album. There was the JLS summer tour to complete too. Manic!

The first day of filming for *The Xtra Factor* was in Birmingham. I was lined up to co-present with Caroline Flack, a gorgeous, great presenter and a lovely person. Me and Caz got into a dressing room and I was expecting some training, a little guidance, as I'd never done TV presenting before, but they just left us there to chat for about twenty minutes, then they came in and said, 'Let's go, let's start!'

'Are you serious?'

I walked out on to the set of *The X Factor* and saw the contestants milling around and it instantly took me straight back to where I was two years ago, but in a good way. I felt very proud, 'cos I was one of the success stories, I'd had my name called out, I'd made it 'all the way', as Dermot said.

But I didn't have long to bask in my success! The producers called me over and it was BANG! Straight into interviewing all the contestants, chatting with hundreds of people, working really long hours in front of the camera. I just learnt on the job, jumped on the camera with Caroline. We had brilliant fun and some really great moments with all these characters.

As I talked to the contestants I saw all the emotions that I had experienced when I was on *The X Factor*, the excitement, the upset, the nerves, the stress. I actually found myself reassuring the rejected ones by saying, 'Come back next year!' I'd always hated it when people said that to me those first two times I'd tried out for the show, but it is true: next year might just be your time. After all, I tried three times.

Me and Caroline had some tough days. We were with each other up to fifteen hours a day, so we had arguments along the way; a few times we interviewed someone and off camera we weren't even talking! That was inevitable under such an extreme schedule but it never lasted, 'cos we are great mates and I loved working with her.

In the lead-up to starting work on *The Xtra Factor*, I'd begun writing songs for my second album. In fact the very first writing sessions were way back before the theatre tour had even started. Two songs surfaced really quickly. 'Heart Skips a Beat' was an immediate candidate for the record and indeed first single. It wasn't actually written for me, and although I'd been given the track for consideration on my first album, at the time we all felt it wasn't the right sound. But this time round I vocalled it and loved it. I still wasn't sure about it as the first single from the album, because it was such a different sound for me, but the more I listened to it, the more I realised what a great song it was. And when Rizzle Kicks jumped in and did their vocal too, that was it, sorted.

Right before the start of the tour I wrote 'Dance With Me Tonight', which would eventually become the album's second single (and my third Number 1). I was really excited about that song and to this day it's my favourite song that I've written. I had so much going on – the tour, the *Xtra Factor* situation, the constant promo – that finding time to write for the new record was very difficult and sometimes it felt like I hadn't written a song for weeks.

By the end of the summer, we were waiting for *The Xtra Factor* to be screened and 'Heart Skips a Beat' was coming out in the first week of September. So once more it was up and down the roads of Britain, radio promo, interviews, just working as hard as I could. My label Sony had three of their own artists competing against each other that week, because alongside mine was a single from Will Young and one from Calvin Harris too. That was a bit puzzling to me, but I wasn't put off, I just kept working, working, working. I rarely got a day off, I was promoting so hard. We were getting great airplay, the YouTube hits were racking up every day for the video (which I loved), Rizzle Kicks were blowing up with their own music, which really helped, and the feedback was really positive, but there was some stiff competition.

The single was due to chart the week that *The Xtra Factor* was first being screened, so I was really anxious to see if my concerns about combining TV presenting and a singing career had been justified all along. Thankfully, I needn't have worried because despite the tough competition, we got the Number 1 slot again, our second chart topper. What a relief!

Strangely enough, although I was obviously over the moon about the Number 1 – I was proper ecstatic – after the initial excitement, I started to feel a bit odd. I didn't feel myself. I couldn't put my finger on why but I started to sense that something wasn't right.

I did a TV show called *8 Out of 10 Cats* that was presented by Jimmy Carr, and I really wasn't myself. After 'Heart Skips a Beat' had hit Number 1, I barely had chance to celebrate 'cos it was straight over to Judges' Houses for *The Xtra Factor*, which involved shoots in Greece, LA and Spain. The new album was coming out in mid-December so there was all of that to complete, and all the promo had just merged into one, without a break. I was exhausted.

It wasn't just the workload. I was anxious about how I'd be received on *The Xtra Factor* – would people like it? Was my music going to be affected? How would I handle the live shows coming up? How would my next new single do? What about the new album? My head was spinning...

Usually with these TV shows the researchers will give you some background on what's going to happen and who's on. Sarah is brilliant at preparing me for anything I do, she puts so much work into making everything right and getting me ready. Amazing. She'd given me all this stuff to read in the green room beforehand but I couldn't face it, I was like, 'Yeah, whatever, I'll just blag it...'

Anyway, I went on the show and the whole thing was a disaster. Not Jimmy or any of the other guests or the show itself, just me. I was rubbish. I wasn't really involved, I hardly said anything, I pretty much just sat there, feeling strange, my head was all over the place. I came off the set and Sarah had a right go at me; she was really cross that I hadn't bothered to do my research and she said it wasn't like me.

Then her and Mark sat me down and said, 'Olly, you haven't been yourself these last few weeks. Tell us what's wrong, we're really worried about you.'

My instant reaction was defensive.

'What do you mean, what's wrong with me? There's nothing wrong with me!'

They said there clearly was, that my attitude to the show that day was totally out of character, that I was fluctuating between being really happy and really moody, and yes, that they were truly worried about me.

I sat there and listened to them shouting and then I just started crying.

For the first time in my career, I was at a point where I just didn't feel happy. I was so drained and down, I wasn't actually enjoying anything I was doing. I was just working, working, working, going along with the schedule, but I wasn't happy. I was *so* tired.

This wasn't the first time I'd screwed up a TV show. A week prior to that we had done *Celebrity Juice* (and a couple of other shows before that too), and you were allowed to drink on-set. I remember getting really drunk, I felt like I just wanted to drink – note that word, 'wanted' to drink. I've never 'wanted' to drink in my life! I enjoy a few beers with the lads like everyone does, but this was different: I wasn't drinking to be sociable or have a nice night out, I *wanted* a drink.

After *Celebrity Juice* I was like, 'Give me another vodka!' and I was necking all these drinks and getting really pissed. I felt like I needed a boost and drinking was that boost a couple of times during this period. But of course the boost didn't last, and when I sobered up I was back to being unhappy again. I didn't understand it: I had a Number 1 record, why was I unhappy?

Back in the dressing room for *8 Out of 10 Cats*, Mark and Sarah were really kind and then Mark was like, 'I think you could be depressed.' I was getting even more defensive now. I was like, 'Me? Depressed? I'm not f**king depressed! Why would I be depressed?'

We chatted in that dressing room for hours and as they explained their concerns I gradually started to become less defensive. I knew what they were saying was fair enough. Looking back, I don't think I was depressed, as it happens: I was just exhausted, worn out, run down. Maybe I was, maybe not, I don't know, but I was sitting there crying in a dressing room even though my career could not have been going any better. Something clearly wasn't right.

Really upset, I said, 'I feel different, I feel like there's something wrong with me, but I don't know why I feel like this. I think the reason is I'm doing too much, it's just got the better of me...'

Instantly Sarah said, 'Well, we can change that!' We chatted and she said we could arrange time off, time to relax, a chance to get my head together, it had all just got on top of me. I know I'm really lucky to do what I do but sometimes with the hours and the travelling, I don't get to see my family and friends as much as I would like to. It can be lonely on the road; sometimes I come offstage after a massive adrenalin rush and then when I go to an empty hotel room on my own it can be an anticlimax. But I love it and I guess that's why I surround myself with a team I get on with – they've become my 'on the road' family and they help me get through the tough moments. Those two difficult weeks around *8 Out of 10 Cats* were the only time in my career that I was cranky and moody. I was like some Jekyll and Hyde character, one minute happy, the next minute really down. I had a bit of a ... well, let's just say I had a low moment there.

15. Just Smile And I'll Be Yours Again

Thanks to Sarah changing my schedule, I was able to get a few lazy days. I went home and got some decent sleep, ate properly, saw my mates, had a couple of nights out with the boys, and just generally recharged. Quite quickly I could feel my spirits lifting each day and it wasn't long before I was raring to go again!

It was just as well that my exhaustion had all come to a head and got sorted because we were due to start the live shows with *The Xtra Factor*. The first show was the best: I was so pumped up, me and Caz were just buzzing. She had a lot going on in her private life at the time because she was dating Harry from 1D, and I was a bit in the middle of it all. It was confusing and hard for her, people were saying things in the press, and it was very difficult. But we got through it and there wasn't one moment when as a team we weren't on it!

An absolute highlight of that series of *The X Factor* was when I got to perform my next single, 'Dance With Me Tonight', on the show. A few weeks earlier when I learnt we'd got the *X Factor* performance, I'd suggested an idea to appear with the Muppets, but almost everyone dismissed it as stupid. However, Tom, my product manager at Epic, was really into the idea and he persisted and within a few weeks was able to turn it around from being an idea that no one wanted to an idea that had to be done! The Muppets had a film coming out in the UK, so it all made sense.

The Muppets came over from the US and rehearsed, and it was an incredible experience seeing the puppeteers bring these characters to life in my performance – just amazing. I was completely star-struck too. That sounds stupid, I know, 'cos I was just talking to a puppet, but when I was performing with Miss Piggy, that's how I felt.

opposite: Posing with The Muppets at rehearsals for our 'Dance With Me Tonight' performance

On the night, I absolutely loved doing the performance and Miss Piggy was on great form. Every year when I go back to perform on *The X Factor*, I wish I was a contestant again. I'd say it's my best-ever *X Factor* performance, and I was delighted to see the papers agree, because they voted me as equal-top performer from the series, alongside Lady Gaga. 'Dance With Me Tonight' is my favourite song and that show was my best-ever performance and I was just so pleased that I had grasped the opportunity to show everyone at *The X Factor* and all the people watching at home that I was an artist now, a singer and a performer. I was delighted.

When it was released as a single, 'Dance With Me Tonight' sold well and initially charted at Number 2. However, it just kept on selling and selling and after three weeks it climbed up to Number 1; it took a while to get there but that song just seemed to appeal to people.

The week after the single came out, my new album, *In Case You Didn't Know*, was released. This had been much harder than my debut record because of my mad schedule kicking off. We only had about twenty-two songs this time, half as many as for my debut, but I felt they were stronger, that my writing was much better, I was more experienced and I had more idea of where I wanted the record to go. I was more involved in the production too, as my label let me get really involved in the entire album. We had come up with a really fantastic record that I think is much better than the first album. The title was a cheeky swipe at people who hadn't heard of me yet, plus of course a title of a song on the album.

In Case You Didn't Know just flew off the shelves. It went to Number 1, achieving double platinum in six weeks. What a great feeling! Then we announced the arena tour for the spring of 2012 and that also started selling really quickly. In fact, by the Christmas of 2011, that massive tour was completely sold out.

So Nick at Epic had been right all along: *The Xtra Factor* had been a good idea after all. Simon seemed happy with my efforts too. At the end of the filming, he came up to me with a present, and when I opened it, he'd given me a framed photograph of himself, signed ... but he'd spelt my name wrong: 'To Ollie...' Cheers, Simon!

No one expects the second album from an *X Factor* finalist to do well. The first album flies, of course, because of all the exposure on telly, but after that the expectation is that interest will have dwindled and the second record will struggle. So getting a Number 1 album with *In Case You Didn't Know* was a very big deal for me.

The week that my album went to Number 1, I didn't know this but a certain someone wanted to ring me. This artist's album had also come out the same week, so they were trying to get Number 1 as well. My tour manager Mark said to me one evening, 'Have you had a phone call?' I'd been told to be available about 5pm but then an interview had come up at the last second so I wasn't able to stick to that unfortunately. Mark said I should check my voicemail. 'Why? Who's trying to call?'

I turned on my phone and went to my voicemails, then heard a familiar Canadian accent.

'Oh my God, Olly, it's Michael Bublé.'

For a second, I thought it was a wind-up.

Shut up!

'Olly, I just wanted to say congratulations on getting Number 1. I worked so hard to get Number 1 too, but you know what? You deserve it, you work so hard. Get some champagne on me and have a great night. Congratulations … you bastard.'

I tried ringing him back but we kept missing each other, then eventually we caught up in his trailer at *The X Factor* final. The reason I tell that story is not to point out that Michael Bublé phones me – which I still find very bizarre! – but to highlight that here you have one of the biggest stars in the world, a man who has sold millions and millions of records, who sells out huge arenas around the world, who is absolutely at the top of his game, and yet even though he was beaten to Number 1, he still had the grace and character to phone and congratulate me. He is genuinely one of the nicest guys you will ever meet, and despite his massive success he is still so down-to-earth and, best of all, he doesn't take himself too seriously. For me to see someone as famous and successful as him behave in such a gracious way is a lesson I will never forget.

After we filmed a video for the third single, 'Oh My Goodness' (which would reach Number 13), it was straight into tour rehearsals. One of the tabloids had published a really horrible picture of me in Barbados – I'd had a great holiday, 'all-inclusive', and I ain't gonna lie, I just ate, ate, ate, so I put loads of weight on! This horrible pap picture showed me with a big belly and I was mortified, so when I came home I got back in shape. I got myself a trainer who beasted me so I was ready for the tour.

I couldn't wait for my first-ever arena tour as a headliner. It was a big set-up, big shows, sold out start to finish. That's what I'd always wanted, an arena tour of my own, and now I'd done it. We were filming a three-part TV documentary too along the way, called *Life On Murs*, so that spiced up events, made things really interesting as we went around the UK meeting fans and going out on day trips doing challenges set by them.

The tour was every bit as unbelievable as I thought it was going to be. The fans were amazing, the responses we were getting were incredible, it was a dream come true. During Boot Camp for *The Xtra Factor*, my sister had had her baby and I'd rushed away from filming to meet him. Little Louis, he's amazing, and that was one of the best parts of the whole year. So for my tour, Mark got my in-ears made up with a little photo of Louis's face: sweet! My voice was strong through the whole tour – my time with the vocal coaches and all the hard work I'd been putting in was paying off and those earlier fears for my voice were in the past.

I had the Brits coming up that month as well. I was nominated for 'Best Single' for 'Heart Skips a Beat', but as much as I wanted to have a great night, the Brits were a strange couple of days. Some people didn't like my performance, and that mixed reaction was quite tough. A few other artists even slagged me off on Twitter, which was disrespectful. The Brits was a big moment for me, it was broadcast to millions of people, a chance to showcase what I was all about. But hey, I gave it my very best, so I can't complain.

Then it was straight back to the tour for the last few of the fifteen dates, and that was just the start of yet another 'busiest year of my life'. In 2012 I have worked across Europe, I've had a Number 1 in Germany, Switzerland and Austria, the album's selling really well in France, Denmark, Sweden, Luxemburg and Poland, so my work is taking me to so many new places that

I might never have even visited before. I've been touring with One Direction in America, which is amazing; I've signed with Columbia in the States and I've been so excited about taking my music there. I've never had any expectations of 'cracking' America but I've always thought I can only ever give everything my best shot and see what happens.

In May 2012, I was asked to fly over to Australia for some promotion as my record was doing really well there too. That was one of the proudest moments of my life. It put it all into context: how far I had come in such a short space of time since I went there with a backpack, as one traveller among thousands. The last time I'd flown there my head had been full of all these thoughts about where my life was heading, what I should do with my future. Back then, I was wondering, how can I achieve my dream? All those things had been a constant thought as I travelled around Australia, hoping that my adventure was the start of something special for me.

And now here I was, getting on a plane again to Sydney, ahead of a promo tour for my own music. Hopefully that trip will also be the start of something special for me again. I only have one regret from this trip Down Under: I just wish I had taken my guitar down the beach, but I didn't have time!

More than three years on from that first Australia trip, I am a completely different person, I live a totally different life now and it's hard to get my head around the changes in my world. When I think back and look at what I've achieved so far – three Number 1 singles, a Number 1 album, sell-out tours, all that – it's amazing to take in how far I've come in such a short space of time. It's almost like two different people.

Remember that line when I first auditioned for *The X Factor*? I said I wanted 'to be a pop star and be famous and sell records and be an international superstar'. When I said those words, I didn't actually believe what was coming out of my mouth, as you now know. Well, I'm not an international superstar, I know that, and perhaps I'll never be one. However, I would say I am an international *singer*, I have sold a lot of records and some people would call me a pop star. I'm currently writing my third album, which I really think will be my best yet, I've got a massive arena tour to play in 2013 and I'm travelling the world singing and promoting my music. That is a great feeling. So in a way those words at that very first *X Factor* audition have come true to some degree. Maybe I did change? Maybe I did become that person?

One thing I have gained in the last three years is a strong belief in myself, I believe in what I can do, I believe in what my voice can do, I believe in my abilities. Don't get me wrong, I still have moments where I doubt myself every day. I know some artists who never doubt themselves, their heads are up their own arses, but that's not me. However, mostly I do – finally – believe in myself.

I know now that I was always supposed to do this, I was born to do this. Even when I was down, when work was so dull and I was struggling to find my direction in life, I still believed that my moment would come at some point, and when it did at that first *X Factor* audition, that totally changed my life.

I'm still very ambitious, I want to keep going. I'm excited about the future and where I am heading. I wanted to change my life and people have helped me to do that by voting for me on *The X Factor*, buying my records, coming to see me in concert. They've been just amazing. I'm lucky enough to have a lot of fans who want to come along for the ride, so let's just see where it takes us!

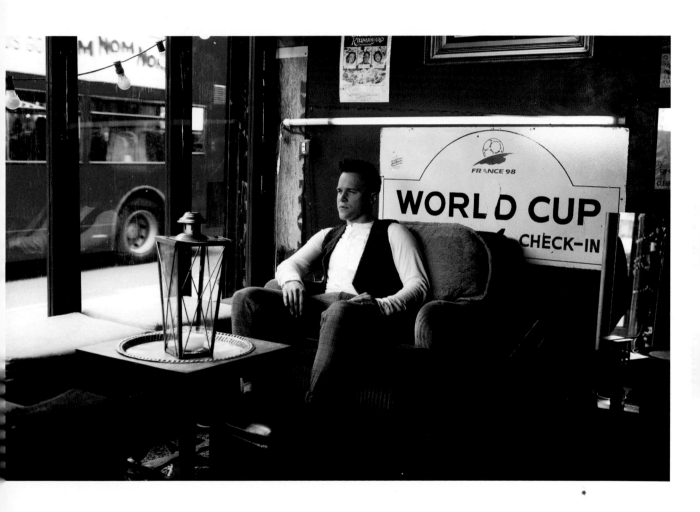

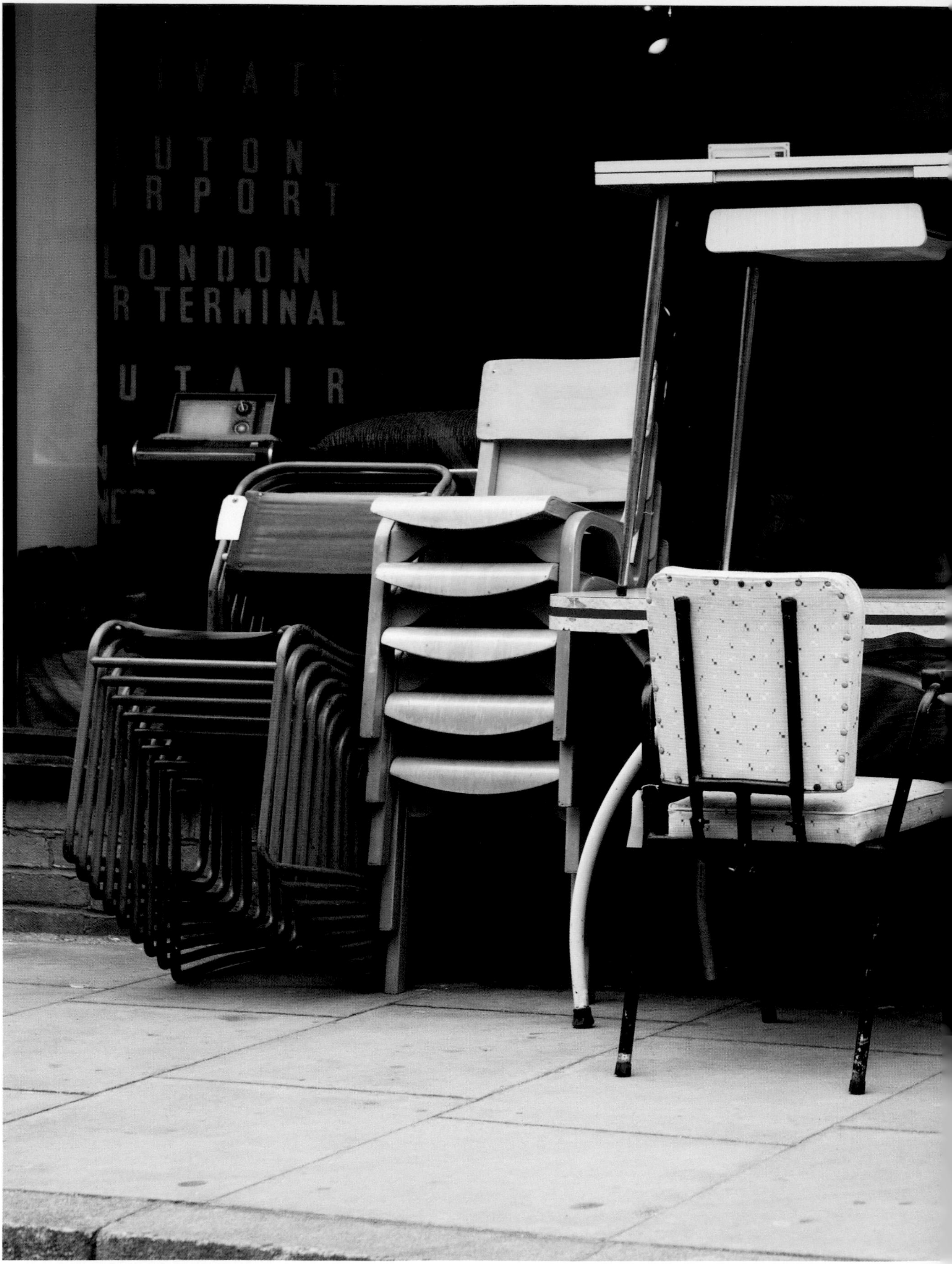

UTON
RPORT
LONDON
R TERMINAL
UTAIR

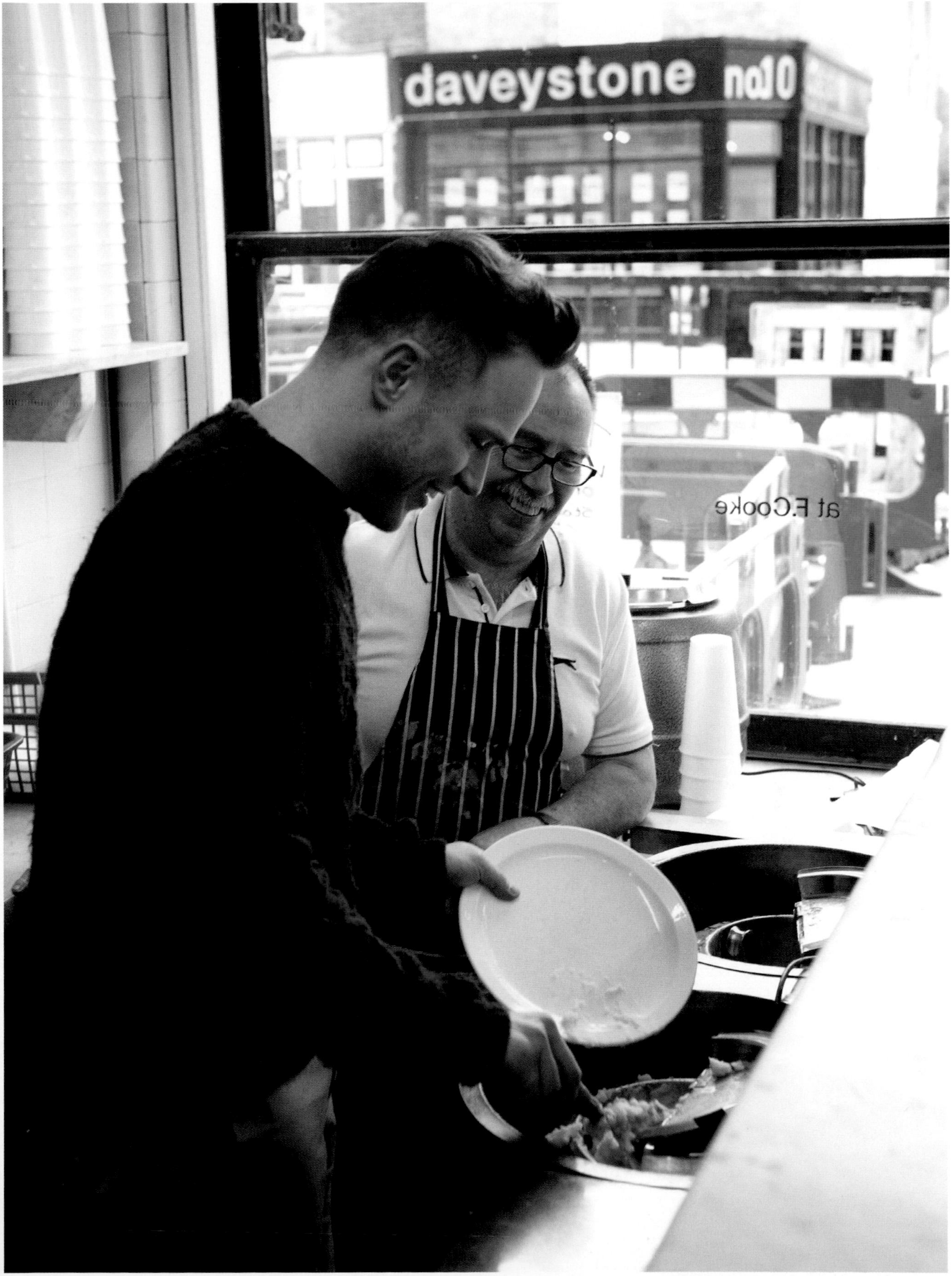
daveystone
no10
at F.Cooke

Thanks

My first book.... crazy! This is something I've always wanted to do since the show, but I felt it wasn't the right time to do it. Now after three years and with all the highs and lows in that time, I felt it was right to tell people what I've been through and the journey I've had in the last six years.

Firstly I want to thank everyone that's been a part of it. Of course all my family for sticking by me through the rough times and the crazy times, Mark Murphy and Sarah Thomas for everything – you both mean the world to me, onwards and upwards! I can't thank Martin Roach enough for sitting with me for hours listening to me rambling away to him, Martin, you must have been sick of me in the end... Hahaha, top guy, let's do it again soon. Dean Freeman – thanks for making me look almost like Brad Pitt in my pictures (ha ha). What a photographer, we wanted the best and we got the best! I love the photos and the way the book looks – thanks to Joby Ellis. A big thanks to Charlotte Hardman for believing that this was worth doing, and to everyone else at Hodder in design, marketing, publicity and sales for all your hard work on making this the best book it could be. Lastly thanks to everyone who has picked up this book to read, I really hope you enjoy it as I genuinely loved every minute of doing it. Now I'm just going to have to sit back and wait to hear your responses online! Hope ya like!

Much love, Happy Days! Olly x

location credits: With thanks to Val Barrett at The Palm Tree, Bow; Speedies, Redchurch Street; Casa Blue, Brick Lane; Cleo's Barbershop, Puma Court; Dave Robinson and Georgie Keen at Repton Boxing Club and Bob Cooke at FF Cookes Pie and Mash shop in Broadway Market

Dean Freeman is an internationally acclaimed photographer and director, who has published 11 books. Bestsellers such as Beckham and Michael Bublé have highlighted Dean's unique ability to create timeless and iconic imagery of musicians, singers, sporting icons and artists – his subjects include Katy Perry, George Michael, David Beckham and Leona Lewis. Dean has also worked with major global brands on advertising campaigns.

Freeman captures a sense of urgency and immediacy, creating a need to look and see his images. His photography has a sense of humour and an appreciation for the absurd, but where Freeman truly excels is in detecting the beauty that extends beyond time and place. –NYLON MAGAZINE

First published in Great Britain in 2012 by Coronet
An imprint of Hodder & Stoughton
An Hachette UK company

2

A CIP catalogue record for this title is available from the British Library
ISBN 978 1 444 76083 5
Printed in Germany by Mohnmedia Mohndruck GmbH, Gütersloh

Hodder & Stoughton policy is to use papers that are natural, renewable and recyclable products and made from wood grown in sustainable forests. The logging and manufacturing processes are expected to conform to the environmental regulations of the country of origin.

Hodder & Stoughton Ltd
338 Euston Road
London NW1 3BH
www.hodder.co.uk